ON FORGIVENESS & REVENGE

ON FORGIVENESS
& REVENGE

Lessons from an Iranian Prisoner

RAMIN JAHANBEGLOO

© 2017 Ramin Jahanbegloo

Printed and bound in Canada at Friesens. The text of this book is printed on 100% post-consumer recycled paper with earth-friendly vegetable-based inks.

COVER AND TEXT DESIGN: Duncan Campbell, University of Regina Press
COPY EDITOR: Caleb Snider
PROOFREADER: Kristine Douaud
COVER ART: *Vintage Cloud and Fog* by David M. Schrader / iStockphoto and *Barbed Wire Fence Detail* by Josef Kubes / iStockphoto.

Library and Archives Canada Cataloguing in Publication
Jahanbegloo, Ramin, author
On forgiveness & revenge : lessons from an Iranian prisoner /
Ramin Jahanbegloo.

(Regina collection)
Includes bibliographical references.
Issued in print and electronic formats.
ISBN 978-0-88977-500-8 (hardcover).—ISBN 978-0-88977-501-5 (PDF).—
ISBN 978-0-88977-502-2 (HTML)

1. Peace—Philosophy. 2. Revenge. 3. Forgiveness. I. Title.
II. Title: On forgiveness and revenge. III. Series: Regina collection

B105.P4J34 2017   172'.42   C2017-905962-9   C2017-905963-7

University of Regina Press
Saskatchewan, Canada, S4S 0A2
TEL: (306) 585-4758 FAX: (306) 585-4699
WEB: www.uofrpress.ca

10   9   8   7   6   5   4   3   2   1

We acknowledge the support of the Canada Council for the Arts for our publishing program. We acknowledge the financial support of the Government of Canada. / Nous reconnaissons l'appui financier du gouvernement du Canada. This publication was made possible with support from Creative Saskatchewan's Creative Industries Production Grant Program.

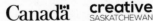

To Azin Moalej

Darkness cannot drive out darkness; only light can do that. Hate cannot drive out hate; only love can do that.

—MARTIN LUTHER KING, JR[1]

Preface

The best way of avenging thyself is not to do likewise.

MARCUS AURELIUS, Meditations[1]

WHEN THE IDEA FIRST CAME TO ME TO WRITE THIS book, it seemed an impossible task. As ridiculous as it may sound, even a decade after my ordeal in the Evin prison I was not sure that I had put my fear, suffering, and grievances behind me. However, one thing seemed certain to me: the 125 days I spent in solitary in an Iranian prison created in me a visceral aversion to violence, hatred, and revenge. I found them pointless and just as repulsive as the horror of solitary itself. Revenge appeared to me as something futile, and I did not and do not consider revenge to be a method of achieving justice. However, one who is hurt commonly thinks of hurting in return, and this is how the desire for vengeance is born. Revenge, there-fore, became an unsurpassable horizon in my thoughts. I thought about it without believing in it. This is why I decided to write about it: not because I like the sound of the word, nor because I believe in the exemplary value of revenge. I consider revenge to be an unnecessary action whose legitimacy is not only useless, but harmful to the human race.

Albert Camus called revenge "a punishment that penalizes without forestalling."[2] The strange thing about revenge is that it can never capture precisely the essence of what it wants and what it does. This cannot be helped: those of us who are vengeful carry the complete truth about our revenge to the grave, though in the end every revenge has its repercussions. All victims of violence and intolerance are well aware of this, for they know that innocence is better than arbitrariness. Nonetheless, I also know that no form of intolerance, harassment, or crime should go unpunished. Such is human justice.

In horrific circumstances, there is a solidarity between human beings: without that solidarity, we are mired in absolute evil. There is, however, also an instance of com-mon awareness of the suffering of victims of aberration and horror, and it is an awareness that defines our civ-ilization in terms of compassion. This opens the door to humanity's magnificent capacity for forgiveness. It

is through this capacity that we humans have to confront our Sisyphean fate of suffering and joy. Perhaps
if we listen attentively for the gentle voice of hope, we
may find it in the image of revenge that has transformed
into forgiveness. I learned this lesson, with difficulty, as
I learned to work past the despair and the disappoint-
ments of life. One may long, as I did, for a moment of
peace: with myself, with my nation, and with humanity.
After my imprisonment, the time of walls was over for
me. I went looking for a door to open in order to free
myself. I expected this freedom to be splendid, and yet it
was a perpetual risk. But things were not always as rosy
for me as they are today. There were times that I didn't
take freedom as seriously as life itself.

In childhood and youth, my ideas about freedom were
undoubtedly naïve. I was naturally a very optimistic person
who believed in the essential goodness of human beings.
I was unprepared for savage politics and for the violence
of solitary confinement, so when I suddenly found myself
confronted with imprisonment I certainly didn't know
how to think about the ugly side of life. Everything turned
out to be different. A gloomy cloud of bitterness and pes-
simism covered my thoughts. My jailers were squeezing
the world to fit their goals, and I had no place in the
world they were shaping: I had not come out of their
ranks, nor out of the womb of the Iranian Revolution. I

was thrust into a drama in several acts without having prepared my lines. It was therefore even harder for me to accept that there are times in all our lives when events create great changes in us and we begin to look at the world and our existence from a new perspective, departing from our previous path. I started thinking about my roots and my ancestors.

I was born in a region of the world—the Middle East—where the notion of revenge is overpowering. One drop is enough to start a tribal feud or a sectarian war. As a result, the idea of revenge and the ideal of forgiveness have preoccupied me since I was a teenager. Fortunately, I was born into a family of forgivers and not among a clan of avengers who sought to take vengeance for injuries or wrongs done to them. However, in Iran, occasions when one could harbour resentment and seek revenge on one's tormentors are not uncommon. Maybe we are born under a sky that seems to be overfilled with violence. Or maybe it is because when we suffer from injustice, we cannot think about anything else: we think about revenge. I soon realized that vengefulness was not an accidental disaster or a horrific interlude in our history: it remained a reality of human existence itself, the terror of which had no beginning and no ending. Fortunately, beyond the frontiers of injustice and revenge lay a splendid happiness of innocent childhood that, under the protective and loving shadow of my parents, counterbalanced the active animosity and bitterness that I breathed in the air. In those days, in the late 1950s and early 1960s, I was far from knowing that would I have to undergo a long and difficult apprentice-ship as the only child of a family that was dominated by the intense reality of tyranny. My father joined the Ira-nian Communist Party in his early twenties. As a young man he was committed to intangible, emotionally charged concepts such as social justice, equality, and freedom. From the moment he started thinking about politics, joining the Communist Party became an instinctive choice for my father. However, Marx and his *Communist Manifesto* did not provide the adequate mode of thinking for my father's inclination toward forgiveness. As a result, he gradually became suspicious of all ideologies and political parties, and he started to store up as much information on Marx-ism as possible until he realized that it was useless for his way to an ethics of forgiveness. He finally found refuge in the thoughts of Muslim mystics and started sharing their thoughts with others. His daily fatigue from Iranian politics, his earlier experience with communist ideology, and the short imprisonment he suffered after the coup d'état of 1953—by the CIA and the British Intelligence Service against the nationalist and popularly elected Prime Minister Mohammad Mossadegh—tended to lock him up in a permanent Stoic attitude toward life. However, my father's Stoic attitude was not merely an ascetic rejection of this world: it was mostly a rebellion against the violence of a shameless reality in which humans were put to suffering and torture.

My father tended to forget his disillusionment with the Iranian Communist Party (Tudeh) after the hardships he and some of his companions had suffered after the coup and the return of the Shah from Rome to Tehran, but his rejection of revenge against the Shah's regime masked a vulnerability, a sense of pride, and a stubbornness. Through all these existential moods ran a beautiful soul that, as time passed, wanted more and more to remain pure of all contact with reality; a soul that was satisfied with the reiteration of a mystical and philosophical approach to forgiveness devoid of all religious content. He came to the conclusion that there was no right side without its reverse, not truth without lie, no good without evil, no light without darkness, and no revenge without forgiveness.

From the very start, my father taught me to think and act in moral terms. He himself became aware of the line that separated revenge and forgiveness through his own father, Mamdali Khan Jahanbegloo. My father's family reflected a balanced mix of Kurds and Azeris. My grandmother was from the Ayrom family. She was related to Muhammad Husayn Ayrom, a senior military leader under Reżā Shah. She was among those who spelled her family name "Ayromlou," using the added suffix "lou." As for my grandfather, he was the descendant of a famous Kurdish tribe, the tribe of Jahanbegloo, which my Turkish friends continue to call it by its Turkic name, "Cihanbeyli," a town and district of Konya Province in the Central Anatolian region of Turkey. My grandfather was very proud of being an Iranian Kurd and had kept all the symbols of his ancestors, notably two swords that were given to him by his own father. I eventually inherited these swords because I was the only son of the elder son of my grandfather. For my grandfather, forgiveness was an art of living. Though a retired military man, he never praised war or violence. As a humanist, he considered revenge as the triumph of evil over good. His house was open to the poor of his neighbourhood: they could come and eat freely at any time. My grandfather and my father both considered the concept that forgiveness should replace revenge in all our decisions in life to be a thoroughly Iranian one. It is true that words of justice and moderation were pronounced for the first time by Zoroaster, an Iranian prophet, but Iranian history, as well as the histories of the Turks and the Arabs, has not always been a realm where excesses and extremes were avoided.

Be that as it may, forgiveness has not yet become a strategy of "living together" for the people of the Middle East. The refusal to take revenge or to legitimate vengeance is the starting point to which the future of the Middle East and the world point us. The question to ask here is, can Americans, Canadians, or Australians have the same sense of horror, disgust, and sorrow when they see images of Syrian, Iraqi, or Palestinian kids blown to pieces by rockets or suicide bombers as when they see acts of terror perpetrated on their own soil? The search for an answer to this question begins with the will to recognize our common humanity and shared values beyond a continuous reinvention of our victimhood and beyond a persistent tendency to blame the other. This is the lesson I learned from my father, as he learned it from his father. For my part, I am fairly certain that I have made the choice to move beyond vengeance. Having chosen, I think that I must state that I wish to be neither a tyrant nor a victim of tyranny. But even more important, I think that I must speak out for forgiveness against revenge. True, in both revenge and forgiveness, the individual is aware of the full and irreducible otherness of the other, but it is only through forgiveness that we can live with the world rather than merely in it. After all, we are dialogical beings, even if we kill and destroy each other. Forgiveness reveals the relationship between individuals that makes dialogue possible. It is the condition for dialogue and is most realized in dialogue. Above all, it presents shared values, especially moral values, as the minimum background that makes dialogue possible in the first place. Yet, even if forgiveness avoids revenge, it has problems of its own in bringing humanity together.

Here too, I must be very clear. I am unequivocally in favour of a forgiving justice, and I would consider its eventual oblivion and collapse a grave misfortune for our contemporary societies. However, I am also deeply persuaded that if we were to forget the horrors of the past, future generations would have to pay for it. As such, the responsibility we bear with regard to the past goes beyond our present time. It is not just a responsibility to those who came before us, but also to those who will come after us. I must start with myself. That is, as quixotic as it may sound, it is my responsibility to talk and write about the hard times we all went through in Iranian prisons. True, I have already written about it, but precisely because my memoirs were read in so many places, it still seems necessary for me to think and write about the ethical outcomes of that experience. The question of ethics has forged ahead of and through me, guiding my thoughts and actions. I was simply pulled forward by ideas of guilt, revenge, forgiveness, and responsibility. It might be that I was swept into writing this book by the urge to find answers to all these questions. Time and time again, I have been persuaded that history is a matter of making moral choices, and those who find themselves confronted with the tragedy of history bear a heightened responsibility to engage in a dialogue with their conscience. Put more clearly, any politics that is not grounded in conscience will hardly save us.

One doesn't need to be a philosopher to understand that violence breeds more violence. The solution to the problem is elsewhere: it is found in the ways we understand violence and seek to deal with it without perpetuating it. I am repeating this basic and self-evident fact for the sake of pointing out that without accepting shared universal moral values, humanity will have no chance to fight the evils of its history. Let us be frank: living in history is not enough; something more is necessary. Perhaps we need to feel that not all lost causes are lost. Time and time again, I have been persuaded of the huge potential for forgiving and not forgetting that exists within human beings. It is just that those who have a duty to awaken this potential mobilize citizens with the worst human qualities: self-interest, greed, fear, and hatred. However, my experience and observations after sixty years is that life is the practice of empathy. I must confess that it is not an easy path to take, nor do I pretend to have taken it, but let us ask the following question: could there be a viable mode of decent life if we continue overlooking empathy as a self-awakening from the nightmares of history? Seen in this light, humanity clearly remains as a promise beyond the blending process of revenge and forgiveness. To a considerable extent, what made me write this book was not the perspective of focusing again on the time I suffered in solitary, but to try to question the "otherness of others" summarized in acts of good or evil. This is an archeological effort to dig deep into the mental geography of humankind. It is this question that has puzzled me from my earliest encounters with philosophy at the age of seventeen.

Like many members of my generation, I was perplexed by the intemperance and excess of emotions created by political circumstances and social associations. The existential and ethical problems raised by my relationships to my parents, professors, friends, lovers, jailers, etc., were almost always accompanied by conceptual problems of both love and hate. I realized very early that, whether shamefully or gloriously, humans are all capable of revenge and forgiveness, perhaps because we are formed by them before we are capable of choosing or rejecting them. I am reminded of the epigraph in an early book of poetry by the Irish poet William Butler Yeats: "In dreams begins responsibility."[3] My dreams and wishes raised questions: Why do we need love? How does love turn into hate? What are we to make of revenge? In what sense can we overcome vengeance with forgiveness?

I suspect today that all these questions are, in a sense, both common and ordinary, although they are rarely raised in relation to our everyday life. Indeed, my central thesis is that questions concerning revenge and forgiveness arise in attempting to live up to our will and wishes, and as a consequence of the failure of ethics and politics in our contemporary world. Given this, an understanding and analysis of what forgiveness is and how it relates to social situations and political circumstances where revenge and resentment are dominant should be central to our present reflections. Unfortunately, in recent decades the issue of who we are, not how we can live together, has become more important in our so-called "global village." In other words, the solid ground of our common values is no longer the question of how we can "be together," but of how to "be oneself." In 1786, the famous British essayist, moralist, and lexicographer Samuel Johnson wrote, "Revenge is an act of passion, vengeance of justice."[4] These words now seem to be taken for granted, with revenge and vengeance both seen as honourable forms of violence that erase dishonour to one's religion or nation. Though vengeance might first appear to be "warm and racy," as it does to Jane Eyre in Charlotte Brontë's novel—"Something of vengeance I had tasted for the first time; as aromatic wine it seemed, on swallowing, warm and racy"—Jane later recognizes, "its after-flavour, metallic and corroding, gave me a sensation as if I had been poisoned."[5] Like vengeance, revenge is also a deadly passion, one whose uncritical acceptance damages the future for human society.

The level of violence in our present world requires us to ask questions about the common values that keep our human civilization together. Taking the long and violent history of "the crooked timber of humanity" into account, Isaiah Berlin once said that the best we could hope for in a "common moral horizon" was what he called a "minimally decent" society.[6] But is even Berlin's minimal hope possible today? Is there any way to build a world of diversity and intercultural dialogue in the face of this politics of universal hatred that renounces recognition of others? All of us seek relief from the frustration caused by globalization and the juxtaposition of cultures it brings with it, which feeds the rise of fundamentalism and transnational terrorism. But we cannot accept the kind of response we see in the killings of the French cartoonists of *Charlie Hebdo* or the November 2015 killings in Paris or the massacre of Pakistani children in Peshawar or the kidnapping of 172 women by Boko Haram in Nigeria. Fanatics and fundamentalists have always rejected and struggled against each other. When fundamentalism seeks to enforce sectarianism through coercion and violence, it invariably leads to terrorism. When people believe that they have the absolute truth, they end up denying other people's existence and can no longer distinguish good from evil. They are thus unable to establish a modus vivendi among different values. Finding a common ground is only possible if we already share enough to recognize that we must behave civilly. If fundamentalism, whatever its form, sanctions violence in its mode of thinking and its methods of acting, it cannot expect to be recognized or tolerated by others. Yet we cannot return to the politics of tyrants, whose motto, like that of the fundamentalists, is "rule unconditionally." To be anti-barbarian in our time is to say "no" unconditionally to fanaticism—not as tyrants or "avenging angels," who are intolerant in their own way, but by engaging in meaningful and empathic dialogue with the otherness of others. Having thus chosen our course with pure purpose, we can renew our trust in forgiveness as a cry from our hearts and minds in the face of revenge.

In other words, fighting the evil of history does not necessarily exclude morality. On the contrary, it gives us strength and the superabundance of restoring forces. In any case, the question remains: what should we do against the plague of revenge with its all-too-human face? To anyone eager to live and to understand, this book offers the agony of those who have tried to answer this question.

1

The stupid neither forgive nor forget; the naive forgive and forget; the wise forgive but do not forget.

THOMAS SZASZ[1]

CIVILIZATION IS A RACE BETWEEN REVENGE AND forgiveness: this is the rule of history. But let us start with some definitions. Revenge is the act of taking vengeance in a spirit of resentment and animosity. As we see throughout human history, it is also a form of retributive punishment or retaliation. Simply put, revenge is like scratching a cat because the cat scratched you. It is an "eye for an eye" morality that escalates violence rather than restoring justice and fairness. Revenge is a negative form of reciprocity marked by the rejection and the destruction of the other. Forgiveness, as opposed to revenge, is a noble sentiment of mutuality accompanied by a sense of empathy and compassion. It is characterized by a series of changes that occur within an individual or a nation wronged by another person or another nation. It is the call of the heart, especially in its relationship with the otherness of the other. Forgiveness is often an individual choice or a political act of abandoning vengeance and resentment, replacing it with reconciliation and tolerance. Forgiving is rediscovering a human dimension of exchange and harmony that adds to the future without changing the past. We learn from history that humankind can never look toward the future if the past is not in the hands of forgiveness. If humanity intends to survive through forgiveness, it must continue fighting its own evil invention—revenge. It should be clear that no one nation, no one individual alone, can win this battle. We should, in this century, therefore ask ourselves how we are to rethink and to achieve in our time, and for all time, the perennial vision of forgiveness. In this time of complacency and conformism, we must lift our eyes to the possibilities and challenges of forgiveness as the hope of tomorrow. History shows us that neither the vengeful nor the fanatic can bring peace and nonviolence to our homes. Instead, they bring pettiness to us and to our world, abandoning our heritage of forgiveness and responsibility. The badge of responsibility in our world is the willingness to seek the path of forgiveness, a very difficult path indeed. The goal of forgiveness, today and tomorrow, must shape our duties and inspire our goals. This ideal is expressed in these words, attributed to Cicero, "Nothing is so praiseworthy, nothing so clearly shows a great and noble soul, as clemency and readiness to forgive."[2]

Revenge and forgiveness are integral parts of the everyday experience of people in the Middle East, as are the creative and dynamic forces of historical change. I was born and raised in Iran, and although I was introduced to many Western and non-Western cultures by spending time in different countries, I consider myself an Iranian with a cosmopolitan background. I also call myself a Middle Easterner and a Muslim. Beyond these labels, I am a person who would like to look at human history and its diverse civilizations and cultures with both gratitude and a critical eye. I agree with G. K. Chesterton when he says, "When it comes to life, the critical thing is whether you take things for granted or take them with gratitude."[3] Not taking anything for granted requires thinking twice about the things of life. It also means trying to learn from our mistakes, at least when we aren't busy justifying them. This, of course, necessitates going far beyond our social roles as politicians, soldiers, writers, academics, artists, doctors, engineers, housewives, or simply fathers, mothers, sisters, and brothers. Identities are parts that people have learned to play as members of a nation, a religion, or a community. With each role we adopt, our behaviour changes to fit the expectations of that nation, religion, or community. In the words of William Shakespeare, "All the world's a stage, And all the men and women merely players: They have their exits and their entrances."[4] I have played my part as a male Muslim born in the Middle East and educated in the West. But, unlike a drop of rain that loses its identity when it hits the ground, human beings do not lose their capacity to think and question while playing their multiple parts.

The essence of the independent mind lies in having the courage to think for oneself. Thinking outside the herd makes the herd seem strange and one who thinks and acts with it a stranger. People have always been concerned about those who are outsiders, as evidenced by much written commentary, both contemporary and ancient. The stranger poses a set of problems for the existing social order; she is not only an outsider but marginal, since she doesn't identify with the system and opposes her individual truth to that of the herd. In *Discipline and Punish*, Michel Foucault writes of the "lyricism of marginality," which, he says, "may find inspiration in the image of the 'outlaw,' the great social nomad, who prowls on the confines of a docile, frightened order."[5]

Moreover, isn't it true that blind faith in the authority of a herd is the worst enemy of truth-seeking? If this is so, then the critical effort to think about values and realities such as revenge and forgiveness requires more than just approving or condemning those values and realities. This unthinking attitude toward joy and pain, in the Middle East in general and in the Muslim world in particular, is found in those who have created fear or have been forced to deal with it. No wonder crowds and dictators hate thinking, but are good bedfellows when it comes to simple words and big lies. As Adolf Hitler insisted in *Mein Kampf*, the masses find it easier to believe big lies, frequently repeated.[6] The tragic side of our human history is that masses have always been misled and misdirected toward violence and revenge, rarely toward forgiveness and coexistence. Crowds need flags and simple words, not thoughts and doubts. They will believe any lie if a voice of authority tells them it is true. In her groundbreaking study of totalitarianism, Hannah Arendt asserts that "the very immensity of the crimes guarantees that the murderers who proclaim their innocence with all manner of lies will be more readily believed than the victims who tell the truth."[7] Lies work the same in every society and in every age. Where can one find the truth in a world that lacks the humility to accept its ignorance and has lost its curiosity for and practice of asking questions about events?

I have had the experience of being right in matters on which the established authorities were wrong, and I paid for my innocence with 125 days of solitary confinement. My prison experiences reminded me of what Henry David Thoreau asserted in beautiful terms: "What I have to do is to see, at any rate, that I do not lend myself to the wrong which I condemn."[8] In doing this, I wish to challenge the injustice that made me and those around me suffer and respond to the idea of the spirit of revenge as the only desirable alternative to suffering. If suffering from an evil act is wrong, fighting that evil with a new form of evil is even more wrong. We are reminded of the challenge Socrates posed to his Athenian friends and followers, recorded in Plato's *Crito*: "Therefore, we should neither retaliate nor treat anyone evilly, no matter what we have suffered from them."[9]

In turning to Socrates' arguments in the *Crito*, I am concerned not merely with the history of philosophy but, more importantly, with the idea that there is a moral obligation to disobey evil without introducing a new evil. The position Socrates takes on this question is exemplified in many opinions on the practice of a just form of civil disobedience. Among these, that of Martin Luther King, Jr. is the most interesting. In his response to the vengeance of the White man in America and the tensions created by African-American resistance to the politics of segregation, King pointed to Socrates: "Just as Socrates felt that it was necessary to create a tension in the mind so that individuals could rise from the bondage of myths and half-truths to the unfettered realm of creative analysis and objective appraisal, we must see the need for non-violent gadflies to create the kind of tension in society that will help men rise from the dark depths of prejudice and racism to the majestic heights of understanding and brotherhood."[10] While King rejected unjust responses to resentment and revenge, he followed Socrates in his commitment to truth and nonviolence. Nonviolence is part of our philosophical culture today because individuals like Socrates and King practiced forgiveness.

My time in solitary confinement in Iran brought me to the belief and conviction that there is forgiveness beyond the horizon of revenge that one experiences in political prisons. Through my experience in solitary and my encounters with the degradation of human beings when they take up the role of torturers and interrogators, I came to clearly understand that the meaning of life must be found beyond acts of barbarity. I arrived at the certainty that the final human ability is the capacity to choose not to fall into the trap of revenge and vengeance. By arriving at this decision, I was challenging not only my own human instincts but the very meaning of a vengeful life. I was reminded of Viktor Frankl's words, "Challenging the meaning of life … is … the truest expression of the state of being human."[11] Prison offered me a rare opportunity to learn the lessons of forgiveness and to study the philosophy of nonviolence, a philosophy that Mohandas Gandhi considered most powerful: "Non-violence is the greatest force at the disposal of mankind. It is mightier than the mightiest weapon of destruction devised by the ingenuity of man."[12] It is difficult to talk about revenge and forgiveness if we do not think in terms of violence and nonviolence. In the same way, there can be no discussion of violence and nonviolence in our world today without involving the notions of revenge and forgiveness. But there are many people around the world who feel that it is futile to talk about non-violence in a world run by greedy and unscrupulous individuals.

Violence is often the result of the human passion for retaliation, but it also often arises from a curious sense of what Francis Bacon called "wild justice,"[13] which is supposed to erase dishonour felt by the self, family, tribe, or nation. If such "wild justice" is taken for granted, as so often is the case in our century, it is a perfect expression of an exchange of evil for evil. Understanding violence in the contemporary world means not only understanding evil but also shedding light on the dialectic of "victims" and "executioners." The closer we get to evil in responding to evil, the more the everyday reality of our individual or collective lives is that of an executioner who either acts out of a personal emotion of hate and revenge or follows an order in the name of a higher authority. As such, a vengeful victim is an executioner who refuses to understand the other, perceiving herself only as a victim of violence. The pain of the victim turns into rage and revenge, and concepts of right and wrong, just and unjust, are abandoned. But a new cycle of violence is not necessarily the outcome of past sufferings. There have been profound changes in human history, notably those that have taken us out of the cycle of violence. When thinking about an end to violence, it is not sufficient just to consider the dialectic of victims and executioners, however important this might be. One must also look beyond the ontology of violence, including its collective dimensions, and try to bring life back to a broken polity. It requires great ethical strength and political wisdom to be able to forgive the evil doers but not forget the evil done. How can an individual or a nation acknowledge the barbarity of an action while calling for a moral transcendence of a tragic event? An end to violence here means an end to the spirit of revenge and vengeance. It also means protecting the victims from a sense of fear that might turn their historical wounds into political weapons of tyranny.

Fear needs no definition. Everyone knows something about fear. Fear is the parent of violence. Perhaps that is why authors like Montesquieu and his disciple Louis de Jaucourt considered fear to be a "tyrannical passion."[14]

The dangerous thing about fear is that it is a communicable disease: others can catch it. The existential fear of the other is always accompanied by a process of "demonization." Demonization feeds on fear and hatred. When demonization becomes acceptable, as part of mainstream public discourse, it creates a climate that is conducive to violence. Why do individuals or nations demonize each other? Because they fear each other. Martin Luther King, Jr. explored this problem of fear of "the other": "They fear each other because they don't know each other; they don't know each other because they have not communicated with each other."[15] King agreed with Gandhi that fear is a fundamental source of evil. But he also agreed with the Mahatma that fear is the opposite of truth. To be truthful, one needs to turn away from fear. This is what King said in his famous speech delivered on the last night of his life, April 3, 1968:

> Well, I don't know what will happen now. We've got some difficult days ahead. But it really doesn't matter with me now, because I've been to the mountaintop … And so I'm happy, tonight. I'm not worried about anything. I'm not fearing any man! Mine eyes have seen the glory of the coming of the Lord![16]

It is not a surprise that King's struggle against segregation in American society went hand in hand with an emphasis on love and overcoming fear. King described love as

> that force which all of the great religions have seen as the supreme unifying principle of life. Love is somehow the key that unlocks the door which leads to ultimate reality. This Hindu-Moslem-Christian-Jewish-Buddhist belief about ultimate reality is beautifully summed up in the First Epistle of Saint John: 'Let us love one another: for love is of God.'[17]

In King's view, to restore a broken community we need to replace the love of power with the power of love. This is founded upon the conviction that *agape* love is "understanding, creative, redemptive goodwill toward all men. *Agape* is an overflowing love which seeks nothing in return. Theologians would say that it is the love of God operating in the human heart."[18] King's ultimate optimism about human nature was based on the conclusion that the validity of nonviolence springs from the Christian concept of *agape* as the only moral absolute. But he also believed in the redemptive possibility of nonviolence in human history and underlined the fact that nonviolent resistance to evil and injustice would produce reconciliation and the Beloved Community. He often described his mission as the pursuit of the Beloved Community: "But the end is reconciliation; the end is redemption; the end is the creation of the beloved community. It is this type of spirit and this type of love that can transform oppressors into friends."[19] In this sense, King's spiritual understanding of the concept of community was in contrast to the individualistic vision of community associated with the social and economic evolution of modernity. King's use of concepts such as solidarity, empathy, and affection as the basis for the Beloved Community takes on greater significance when considered in the context of a radical transformation of human connectedness and the self-organization of society. In proposing such change, King infused the concept of *agape* love into the idea of the interrelated life.

In 1958, King wrote, "*Agape* is not a weak, passive love. It is love in action. *Agape* is love seeking to preserve and create community. It is insistence on community even when one seeks to break it ... It is a willingness to go to any length to restore community."[20] As a result, King's vision of a reconciled society was that of an inclusive community with a sense of responsibility: "At the heart of all that civilization has meant and developed is 'community'—the mutually cooperative and voluntary venture of man to assume a semblance of responsibility for his brother."[21] King's conception of "reconciliation" is best described as a state of total connectedness and a network of reciprocity. The recognition of one's indebtedness and one's responsibility to others leads, in King's philosophy, to an awareness of the interdependent character of life: "In a real sense, all life is interrelated. The agony of the poor impoverishes the rich; the betterment of the poor enriches the rich. We are inevitably our brother's keeper because we are our brother's brother. Whatever affects one directly affects all indirectly."[22] King's conception of a reconciled society does not appear to have room for an individual good that can be opposed to the common good. In other words, the self cannot truly be ignorant of others within the community. This idea is based mainly on the fact that mutual recognition and reconciliation embody a sense of inclusiveness and a sense of mutual dependence among the members of the community.

It is interesting to note that King's notion of inclusiveness is an intercultural imperative rather than a mono-cultural sense of belonging. King proclaimed, "All men are interdependent. Every nation is an heir of a vast treasure of ideas and labor to which both the living and the dead of all nations have contributed."[23] That is to say, King's vision of the Beloved Community brings together the two themes of emancipation and self-transformation.

But King was also very attentive to the Gandhian concept of "suffering" as a nonviolent mode of resistance against oppression and injustice. For King, suffering is more powerful than violence in persuading an opponent of his or her wrongdoing:

> I've seen too much hate to want to hate, myself
> … and every time I see it, I say to myself, hate
> is too great a burden to bear. Somehow we must
> be able to stand up against our most bitter oppo-
> nents and say: "We shall match your capacity to
> inflict suffering by our capacity to endure suffer-
> ing. We will meet your physical force with soul
> force. Do to us what you will and we will still
> love you … but be assured that we'll wear you
> down by our capacity to suffer, and one day we
> will win our freedom. We will not only win free-
> dom for ourselves; we will so appeal to your heart
> and conscience that we will win you in the pro-
> cess and our victory will be a double victory."[24]

2

I am hopeful, despite the enemy, in the day of judgement
His gift of forgiveness will not burden me with sins!

HÂFEZ[1]

FOR HUMAN BEINGS LIKE MARTIN LUTHER KING, JR.
and Mohandas Gandhi, there is something significant
to be gained by being able to suffer for others. Here we
find the whole distinction between ethics and politics.
To talk about ethical obligation is to underline the otherness of the other. Politics, however, is not concerned
explicitly with the other, unless ethical obligation requires
the acknowledgement of others in the political arena. As
such, while politics appears more than ever to be a form of
management and decision-making, ethics is imperatively,
as the French philosopher Emmanuel Levinas affirms in
Ethics and Infinity, a call by the other.[2] Politics is the process of weighing and organizing the competing actions

of a plurality of others, but the otherness of the other is never a priority in the political realm. By contrast, the ethical imperative is not a political necessity. It is always relative to, and in dialogue with, the otherness of the other. At this point, it is crucial to remember that the ethical proceeds in a responsive and responsible manner by saying, "No" to any form of violence. According to Levinas,

> The face is what one cannot kill, or at least it is that whose *meaning* consists in saying: 'thou shalt not kill.' Murder, it is true, is a banal fact: one can kill the other; the ethical exigency is not an ontological necessity. The prohibition against killing does not render murder impossible, even if the authority of the prohibition is maintained in bad conscience about the accomplished evil— malignancy of evil. The prohibition also appears in the Scriptures, to which the humanity of man is exposed in as much as it is engaged in the world. But to speak truly, the appearance in being of these 'ethical peculiarities'—the humanity of man is a rupture of being. It is significant, even if being resumes and recovers itself.[3]

The face of the other cannot prevent violence, but it can call into question the self and make it acknowledge ethical responsibility and justice. We can even say that ethics is a call to responsibility in politics: Levinas's "ethical exigency" is the ultimate tribunal to which the political can appeal in order to prevent evil from coming to power. Let us notice here that evil as embodied in murderous politics necessarily offends every version of ethical exigency. It also obviously offends the basic Aristotelian notion of civic friendship as an authentic political action.

Aristotle distinguishes between civic friendship (politike philia) and friendship in its personal form. As Aristotle beautifully defines it, being friends with someone civically means, "wishing for him what you believe to be good things, not for your own sake but for his, and being inclined, so far as you can, to bring these things about."[4] As such, friendly civic relations are a necessary element of a just society. Unfortunately, we moderns totally dismiss Aristotle's view of the role of friendship in political relations by claiming that it holds solely for the ancient world and not for ours. We have moved quite far from the Aristotelian conception of politics. The Athenians, particularly a philosopher like Aristotle, would have found our ways of doing politics too corrupt and lacking in virtuous telos. In our world, politics by its very nature is no longer the art of organizing society, but the art of achieving revenge. Populism is revenge against democracy, and neo-liberalism is revenge against communism and all forms of the welfare state. More than that, a Joseph Stalin or an Adolf Hitler lurks inside every politician whose only political aim is to gain and to consolidate power. Stalin and Hitler had enormous capacities for organizing political revenge. Both harboured feelings of revenge and resentment that were just waiting for a chance to reveal themselves in acts of cruelty and madness. Stalin and Hitler made themselves indispensable to the Russian and German peoples, whose resentment they embodied, seeming to transform and transcend their people.

Political resentment comes into being for specific reasons. Far from being the product of dark satanic forces, it appears when and where the public realm is stripped of its ethical foundations. We must therefore meet the politics of revenge where it matters most: in crowds. It has become clear to some that there exists a thin line between crowds and violence, perhaps because crowds, once they become self-aware, claim to know where right and wrong are to be found. It is always in the name of "good" and "bad" or "right" and "wrong" that crowds around the world are capable of making blood flow.

According to Gustave Le Bon in *The Psychology of Crowds*, "Crowds are somewhat like the sphinx of ancient fable: It is necessary to arrive at a solution of the problems offered by their psychology or to resign ourselves to being devoured by them."[5] We need to be aware of the model of politics that counts on the numbers in crowds and not necessarily on the intelligence of the individual. Most of history's great political tragedies and cruelties were the result of the domination of numbers over spirit. For the Danish philosopher Søren Kierkegaard, the "dialogical" manner of being was in opposition to what he called the "numerical" mode of existence: for Kierkegaard, the individual is always against the crowd. "Wherever the crowd is, untruth is," proclaims Kierkegaard in a draft of his dedication to *Upbuilding Discourses in Various Spirits*, because the crowd destroys the individual's capacity to make decisions and makes the individual totally irresponsible.[6] According to Joachim Garff in *Søren Kierkegaard: A Biography*, when thousands demonstrated in the streets of Copenhagen in 1848 to demand labour reforms and constitutional government, Kierkegaard noted in this journal that "every movement and change that takes place with the help of 100,000 or 10,000 or 1,000 noisy, grumbling, rumbling, and yodeling people ... is *eo ipso* untruth, a fake, a retrogression .... A mediocre ruler is a much better constitution than this abstraction, 100,000 rumbling nonhumans."[7] Kierkegaard absolutely hated the idea of government of the crowd, by the crowd, and for the crowd. Yet his fear of the possible authoritarian outcome of group rule did not prevent him from considering responsible dialogical citizenship.

The Kierkegaardian subject is not a monological individual who oscillates between the false either/or of a possessive individualism (which claims that I can find my identity in my private sphere) and a radical consensualism (which leaves no space for the existential self-choice of the subject). Kierkegaard is in favour neither of individualist atomism nor of any kind of social holism. The true Kierkegaardian either/or is that of an opposition between moral individualism and fundamentalism. This gives the Kierkegaaardian individual a kind of an anti-totalitarian reflex. The ethical self-understanding of the Kierkegaardian self does not belong absolutely to the inward perspective of the individual. Individual ethical continuity provides the individual with an intensification of her self-choice. In self-choice, the individual discovers her self-activating principle while in the world. Self-choice is not necessarily a choice between good and evil, but rather a choice to exist as a dialogical self who is capable of sustained ethical judgment. As Kierkegaard affirms admirably in *Either/Or*, "The greatness is not to be this or that but to be oneself."[8] Choosing oneself takes place prior to value conflicts. It is the existential condition of the ideal possibility of entering a dialogical actuality. Kierkegaard's dialogical either/or provides a correction to arbitrary modes of either/or that present forms of non-choice. His defence of radical self-choice presents the individual with a well-formed identity and provides a check and balance for the totalitarian drives that threaten freedom. This is a leitmotif that runs from Kierkegaard's *Either/Or* to today's anti-totalitarian and anti-fundamentalist dissent. *Either/Or*, as the title implies, is obviously about choice, but it is also about the possibility of change, not only from the aesthetic to the ethical and from the ethical to the religious, but also change that aims at achieving the equilibrium necessary to move against a fundamentalist view of faith and life.

As we have seen time and again, the idea of revenge draws an enthusiastic crowd. There is an interest in many countries in public executions. Take the example of Iran, which puts more people to death than any other country except China, where people gather in the streets to watch the hanging of their fellow human beings. According to human rights organizations around the world, more than 687 individuals were executed in Iran in 2013. This, the ultimate in cruel, inhuman, and degrading social action perpetuates a culture of acceptance of violence. Witnessing public executions has both short- and long-lasting psychological effects on individuals, especially children. Several children have died in Iran as a result of re-staging public executions as part of a game. In the case of public executions, the crowd always takes a sadistic pleasure in witnessing what Albert Camus calls "the most premeditated of murders," thinking in terms of such action as a legalized form of revenge.[9] The death penalty in Iran is a legal way of banalizing violence through an act of vengeance. It is shedding the blood of a wrongdoer for the sake of its deterrent effect on the future wrongdoers. But George Bernard Shaw argue in his preface to *Androcles and the Lion* that "[s]acrificing a criminal to propitiate God for the murder of one of his righteous servants is like sacrificing a mangy sheep or an ox with the rinderpest: it calls down divine wrath instead of appeasing it. In doing it we offer God as a sacrifice the gratification of our own revenge and the protection of our own lives without cost to ourselves; and cost to ourselves is the essence of sacrifice and expiation."[10] The death penalty is not the justice of the upright but the revenge of barbarism against civilization.

The mob is the vortex within which the balance between politics and revenge whirls. Let us take, for example, the role played by the mob in contemporary Iranian history. A local gang leader, Shabān Jafari, known as Shabān Bimokh ("Brainless"), played a role in the coup of 1953 and later in Moḥammad Reżā Shah's regime, which superbly illustrates the use of revenge to impose social control and achieve mob rule. In August 1953, when the Shah finally agreed to overthrow the nationalist government of Mohammmad Mossadegh with the help of the British Intelligence Services and the CIA, Shabān

Jafari and his street thugs played an instrumental role in creating chaos on the streets of Tehran and fighting the opponents of the coup d'état. In this context, crowd psychology can be considered the principal generator of social hostility and political violence. There are many examples of mob psychology in modern and contemporary times. The barbaric history of lynching in America is the story of revenge committed outside the boundaries of due process by a frantic mob. The word "lynching" comes from the name of Charles Lynch, a landowner in Virginia in the late eighteenth century who frequently held illegal trials on his property and whipped the accused. Over time, lynching came to refer to all forms of violent citizen vigilantism. The crowd not only witnesses the act but acts as a judge and perpetrator of violence. The victims, usually Black Americans, were beaten, whipped, burned, dismembered, and hanged. In Fritz Lang's first American film, *Fury* (1936), an innocent man, Joe Wilson (Spencer Tracy), is nearly lynched by an angry mob. Lang is not interested in reproducing the reality of violence in American society. On the contrary, as a visionary filmmaker, he uncovers the instinct for revenge in the mob and in the victim. Tracy's character, Joe, who begins the film as a gentle and considerate man, emerges from his near-death experience as a man consumed by resentment and revenge. The main perpetrators are brought to trial for murder, and

Joe is determined to make his would-be murderers pay. However, tormented by conscience and persuaded by his fiancée, Katherine Grant, Joe walks into the courtroom and demonstrates his moral fitness in opposition to the tyranny of the mob:

> I don't care anything about saving them. They're murderers. I know the law says they're not because I'm still alive. But that's not their fault. And the law doesn't know that a lot of things that were very important to me, silly things, maybe, like a belief in justice and an idea that men were civilized and a feeling of pride that this country of mine was different from all others. The law doesn't know that those things were burned to death within me that night.[11]

Joe Wilson's narrative of revenge is overcome by his conscience and sense of guilt. He runs away from his taste for revenge with a sense of guilt that lights his way to the future. Lang's *Fury* shows us that revenge, rather than fixing matters, destroys everything it touches. In Shakespeare's revenge tragedies, murderers and tyrants are always overwhelmed by a sense of guilt. Macbeth's guilt-driven madness leads him to collapse and death. The intensity of Lady Macbeth's guilt, revealed in her cry of

"Out, damned spot! Out, I say,"[12] remains even through her extreme confusion and delusion. In guilt, as in life, every revenge has an equal and opposite reaction. In the end, the vengeful always fall.

3

It is better to be violent, if there is violence in our hearts, than to put on the cloak of nonviolence to cover impotence.

MOHANDAS GANDHI[1]

A CONSCIOUS ACT OF REVENGE IS ALWAYS ACCOM-panied by an opposite sense of guilt. Anyone who has been involved with social tensions has confronted the problem of guilt. The feeling of guilt motivates social actors to submit to ethical judgment and to accept punishment for their wrongdoings, and invites citizens to reflect more profoundly on how vulnerable a polity is to ethical corruption and evil. Strangely, the ethical reaction of guilt is the result of the same moral code that fails to give us guidance when we find ourselves confronting evil in politics. We might say that this deficiency means we are free to decide as we please, letting the moral code take the blame for its failure to give advice in the real world, the world in which we must make choices. However, the moral legitimacy of democratic institutions depends primarily on the ethical stubbornness of citizens who refuse to compromise their moral integrity, even for the sake of an important practical end. French political philosopher Pierre Manent describes democracy as an act of will: "Democracy aims to have its citizens go from a life that one suffers, receives, and inherits to a life that one wills. Democracy makes all relations and all bonds voluntary."[2] There is an understanding of voluntary engagement here that implies a responsible refusal to destroy political life. Each person's moral commitment is, in this sense, a commitment to a vision of what a socially cohesive democratic society should be. This claim is particularly pertinent in dealing with the politics of guilt and in balancing the ethical bonds that enable citizens to live and share together. As such, our commitment to uphold ethical values reinforces those values within a political community. In other words, a commitment to ethical values requires a commitment to their political expression and public display. Guilt denotes the failure to uphold an ethical bond in the shared life of a moral community. The more guilty the individual, the more that individual stands apart from the public realm that involves a shared sense of responsibility. For Hegel, it is the loss of such a shared sense of responsibility that gives rise to the idea that one should "flee from contact with the actual world."[3] However, though guilt is a form of rupture with the community, it also reveals and discloses who an individual is. This revelatory character of guilt reveals that each subject is indissolubly bound to the offense that he or she has committed. Through guilt, what was done in the past is repeated as a desire to repair the damage suffered by the other. The subject seeks to restore and repair the injured party by bearing the burden of the other's suffering. Guilt is, therefore, a responsible reply to the other that offers the possibility of understanding a shared community through the eyes of the victims rather than the victors.

Hegel explores this experience of guilt as felt by the individual in his reading of Sophocles' *Antigone*. As Hegel puts it, in assuming the boundaries between family and polis and then transgressing the political laws of Athens, Antigone "disturbs the peaceful organization and movement of the ethical world."[4] In *Antigone's Claim: Kinship Between Life and Death*, Judith Butler insists that Antigone as a transgressor of the polis establishes a "law beyond law … A law that emerges as the breaking of the law … not a law of the unconscious but some form of demand that the unconscious necessarily makes on the law, that which marks the limit and ambition of the law's generalizability."[5] Establishing such a law transforms the basis of guilt. In Hegel's approach, the ambiguity of guilt remains—there is little doubt that Antigone is guilty since she turns away from one ethical sphere in favour of another. In this case, guilt is an expression of the subject devoting herself to one ethical sphere and transgressing it for another. Creon also suffers from a sense of guilt because he fails to prevent the polis from moving forward to another ethical sphere. Creon's acknowledgement of his guilt is a form of self-destruction: "And the guilt is all mine—can never be fixed on another man no escape for me. I killed you, I, god help me, I admit it all!"[6] Creon feels the destruction of his very being upon suffering guilt. This leads Hegel to add that Creon "surrenders his own character and the reality of his self, and has been ruined. His being consists in his belonging to his ethical law, as his substance; in acknowledging the opposite law ... it has become an unreality."[7]

By comparing the cases of Antigone and Creon, we can distinguish between two forms of guilt: on the one hand, a guilt that is negative and brings shame and destruction (that of Creon), and on the other hand, a guilt that is positive and takes the form of a responsible response to the suffering of the other (that of Antigone). It is this latter form of guilt that embodies the full meaning of the German word *Schuld*, which means simultaneously bond, obligation, and debt to the other. Antigone's deep sense of guilt corresponds to her indebtedness to the polis as an ethical structure. So, unlike the negative guilt of Creon, which is a pathway to despair, the positive guilt of Antigone is an attentiveness to the logic of togetherness of the polis. This attentiveness to intersubjectivity and the ethical value that can arise from it is both an epistemic moment and an ethical moment. In authoring one's actions, one also becomes answerable for the sense of guilt that can result from them. I would suggest that it is with such epistemic humility that one's responsible responsiveness to the irreducible appeal of the other turns toward the acknowledgement of guilt as an ethical stance. Guilt in this scenario carries with it the fundamental idea that one has the potential not only to create evil but to repair it by being susceptible to the suffering of the other. As George Eliot's Dorothea proclaims in *Middlemarch*, "I believe that people are almost always better than their neighbours think they are."[8]

Instead of suggesting a uniform sense of guilt as the source of a recognition of moral values, we can distinguish between guilt as considered by community ethics and guilt that is closely related to an ethics of fraternity. While it is true that a sense of guilt is a source of awareness of values in both forms of ethics, it is questionable whether it is the same kind of guilt. Unlike the tragedy of *Oedipus*, which, like *Antigone*, represents the division of the polis against itself and the sense of guilt that follows, the murder of Abel by Cain illustrates hatred between brothers and a transgression against the kingdom of God. This model of biblical fratricide is completed with the story of Joseph and his brothers and finds its solution in community ethics. When Joseph finally discloses his identity and is reunited with his brothers, he tries to give his entire story some purpose and relieve his brothers' guilt for selling him into slavery by saying that God had put him in Egypt to preserve his family in the famine. The sense of guilt that follows the failure of the ethics of fraternity is corrected by the logic of a highly developed community ethics. The effects of fratricidal guilt resulting from violent and harmful tendencies toward one's brother or neighbour are compensated for and disguised by the imperatives of community ethics. The sense of guilt, however, remains in the chamber of community memory as an open door that leads the community not into a place beyond the law, but into the heart of the law. Guilt, with its ethical and communitarian consequences, is recalled as a transformed relationship to the world. This explains why Paul Ricoeur affirms that the experience of guilt brings about a veritable revolution of consciousness because, with it, "what is primary is no longer the reality of defilement, the objective violation of the interdict, or the vengeance let loose by that violation, but the evil use

of liberty [*liberté, Freiheit, freedom*] felt as an internal dim-
inution of the value of the self."[9] Guilt, then, announces
the existence of a new dimension of consciousness: the
radical development of a personal moral responsibility,
or what Ricoeur calls the "it is I" who is responsible for
this evil. As such, the sense of guilt (*Schuldgefühl*) brings
about a phenomenological transformation of the subject.
This phenomenological disclosure of the structure of guilt
closely parallels Karl Jaspers' account of guilt as in the
moral, not the ontological, sphere of analysis.[10]

In *Die Schuldfrage*, Jaspers develops a schema that distinguishes between four kinds of guilt: criminal guilt,
political guilt, moral guilt, and metaphysical guilt. Criminal guilt has to do with transgressions of law within a
particular legally constituted jurisdiction. Political guilt
deals with the culpability of political actors for crimes
committed by the state. Jaspers carefully distinguishes
political guilt from collective guilt, which is the co-respon-
sibility of a nation for the acts committed by its regime.
Moral guilt has to do with an individual's personal sense
of culpability. "The morally guilty," writes Jaspers, "are
those who are capable of penance, the ones who knew, or
could know, and yet walked in ways which self-analysis
reveals as culpable error—whether conveniently closing
their eyes to events, or permitting themselves to be intox-
icated, seduced, or bought with personal advantages, or

obeying from fear."[11] Last, but not least, what Jaspers calls metaphysical guilt is the failure to demonstrate solidarity with the idea of a universal humanity when humanity is threatened. In the case of the surviving citizens of post-Nazi Germany, it is the humiliation of "being alive," whether they happened to be Jewish or not. Jaspers' notion of metaphysical guilt ultimately requires a relationship between the subject and humanity. The notion of metaphysical guilt, understood within the parameters of Jaspers' philosophy, thus requires that "we further feel that we not only share in what is done at present—thus being co-responsible for the deeds of our contemporaries—but in the links of tradition."[12] As mentioned previously, Ricoeur's response to Jasper's *Schuldfrage* is that "guilt demands that chastisement itself be converted from vengeful expiation to educative expiation and amendment."[13] For Ricoeur, human conscience needs to "understand its past condemnation as a sort of pedagogy."[14]

This capacity for change and self-education is what Martin Buber calls "self-illumination." In his essay "Guilt and Guilt Feelings," Buber describes existential guilt as a necessary stage in human relationships because it can help people restore the human order of justice and undo the harmful effects of failed responsibilities: "Existential guilt occurs when someone injures an order of the human world whose foundations he knows and recognizes as those of his own existence and of all common human existence."[15] In clearly distinguishing existential guilt from neurotic guilt, he insists on the illuminating task of conscience as a call for reconciliation. According to Buber, reconciliation helps the injured individual overcome the consequences of guilt and restore trust and justice:

> Each man stands in an objective relationship to others; the totality of this relationship consti- tutes his life as one that factually participates in the being of the world. It is this relationship, in fact, that first makes it at all possible for him to expand his environment into a world. It is his share in the human order of being, the share for which he bears responsibility. An objective rela- tionship in which two men stand to one another can rise, by means of the existential participation of the two, to a personal relation; it can be merely tolerated; it can be neglected; it can be injured.[16]

In a sense, the experience of guilt is a process that occurs when someone injures the order of the human world, but it also takes on the responsibility to repair that injury. In other words, without a sense of guilt, without a desire to repair the injury caused to another, there would be no dialogue. The guilty man re-enters a dialogue with the world and by the same token is seized by the higher power of conscience. One learns from one's sense of guilt to know the limits of one's knowledge, the extent of one's power, and the fact that one has no control over the world. The dialogical dimension of guilt adopts a posture of epistemic humility in order to draw upon the wider spectrum of human experience rather than a singular self-establishing discourse that asserts superiority and hegemony. Guilt is therefore distinct from shame.

Both feelings of guilt and feelings of shame are involved in conscience. However, as John Rawls asserts, "In general, guilt, resentment, and indignation invoke the concept of right, whereas shame, contempt, and derision appeal to the concept of goodness."[17] Shame helps us to recognize the human potential for barbarism. According to Hannah Arendt, "this elemental shame, which many people of the most various nationalities share with one another today, is what finally is left of our sense of international solidarity."[18] Arendt thus shows us that we cannot pretend that we are guilty for the suffering of others while ignoring the political reality that we live in a shared world. The politics of guilt, therefore, is not to be confused with an abstract and individualistic conception of responsibility. On the contrary, it expresses the idea that we share a common world that includes both those implicated in the wrongdoing and those wronged. As

such, the burden of guilt—namely, the irreversible consequence of our actions and the socio-historical context in
which they take place—is not only a *moral* idea but also
a *political* one. It would not be wrong to argue that guilt
assumes a shared ground of values and a feeling that we
are dependent on the presence of others, be they real or
imagined. It is a moral sentiment that addresses an essential component in our political life. But it also refers to
the civic responsibility that we must assume as citizens
of a human world. It is true that this responsibility might
not turn us into better human beings, but it implies the
human ability and willingness to transcend self-interest
and set aside oneself for the sake of others while striving
for one's own self-realization, a concept so well expressed
by Mohandas Gandhi: "All humanity is one undivided
and indivisible family, and each one of us is responsible
for the misdeeds of all the others."

4

Man has set for himself the goal of conquering the world but in the process loses his soul.

ALEKSANDR SOLZHENITSYN[1]

OUR CENTURY HAS BEEN CHARACTERIZED AS VENGE-ful, and not without reason. We cannot grasp the essence of violence in the contemporary world without recognizing that revenge and resentment are still capable of untold cruelties. There is no more important problem facing the world today than how to deal with the politics of revenge, and there is no nonviolent response to it more important than that characterized by the idea of forgiveness. However, the moment we start thinking about and questioning the nature of this problem and the response to it, we begin to realize how difficult it is to address it, both philosophically and politically. Philosophers, writers, and reformers have spent days, months, and years exploring the true nature of revenge and resentment and whether forgiveness is the right response. Unfortunately, humanity has not given up being vengeful in its thoughts and actions. Paradoxically, the history of human existence has also been a narrative of the art of compassion and a desire to forgive in the name of justice.

It is anything but a new insight to recognize that hatred begets hatred and vengeful action violates our most fundamental notions of right and wrong. In the West alone, three of the greatest authors of modern times, Shakespeare, Dumas, and Melville, have brought the problem of revenge out of theology into the world of human action. "Let's make us medicines of our great revenge, to cure this deadly grief," says Malcolm in Act 2, Scene 3, of *Macbeth*.[2] Macduff goes on to commit an act of revenge against Macbeth. *Hamlet* is also a revenge tragedy, but the main character is unable to avenge the murder of his father. Unlike the characters in *Macbeth*, he finds himself alone with his doubts and weaknesses. And yet, Hamlet gives his reasons for revenge:

> Does it not, think thee, stand me now upon—He that hath killed my king and whored my mother, Popped in between th' election and my hopes, Thrown out his angle for my proper life, And with such cozenage—is't not perfect conscience?

To quit him with this arm? And is't not to be
damned, To let this canker of our nature come
in further evil?[3]

Hamlet deals with "moral revenge" rather than "physical revenge." Unlike Brutus in *Julius Caesar*, Hamlet is neither a public avenger nor a political assassin. While Hamlet has scruples against physical revenge, Brutus is a noble Roman who is aware of the "providence of some high powers that govern us." Hence, his hands are stained with blood in the name of Republican Rome. Republican revenge is complete at the Battle of Philippi when Brutus meets the ghost of Caesar and exclaims, "Oh, Julius Caesar, thou art mighty yet. Thy spirit walks abroad, and turns our swords in our own proper entrails."[4] Shakespearean tragic characters often become aware of their inner existential dilemmas in relation to the problems of revenge and guilt, which is part of the reason we continue to identify easily with Shakespearean characters who, like Macbeth and Hamlet, face moral and psychological challenges in the pursuit of revenge.

Shakespeare had a good sense of the balance between revenge as a self-protective disguise and the vindication of forgiveness without revenge. The former involves a sentiment that always accompanies a particular experience of victimization, but this victimization process may also be motivated by pride, envy, or simply resentment.

It can be very difficult to accept forgiveness as a primary goal in cultures and societies in which the drive for revenge is overpowering. This is especially true if the claims of honour and a sense of retaliation and retribution are stronger than the desire for social harmony and political exchange. Unfortunately, many do not accept the idea of forgiveness as a way to channel vengeful impulses in human societies, which means that our sense of the proper scope and function of revenge dictates much of our attitude toward the idea of justice. The result is usually a passionate retaliation for past wrongs suffered by the person resorting to revenge. As in the case of *Othello*,[5] the revenger may be a tragic hero whose revenge is an attempt to vindicate purity and chastity. Othello strives to act with fairness and love, and because justice is so important to him, he must convince himself that he is not an agent of revenge. Like Hamlet, he struggles against his urge for revenge and does not welcome the idea of assassination. Indeed, he observes, "So sweet was ne'er so fatal. I must weep, But they are cruel tears. This sorrow's heavenly, It strikes where it doth love … I that am cruel am yet merciful; I would not have thee linger in thy pain."[6] Othello is an "honorable murderer."[7] His revenge takes the form of a ritual murder, with the same psychology that we find today in the case of honour killings. Honour killing is a form of family revenge. Worldwide, two thirds of female victims are killed by their families, and fathers or brothers are involved in more than one third of these murders. According to multiple studies, 44 per cent of honour killings in the Muslim world and 91 per cent in North America were related to the unacceptable "westernization" of women.[8] The level of barbaric revenge shown in such honour killings often resembles some of the murders in Shakespeare's *Titus Andronicus*.[9] With its ritual sacrifice, bodily mutilation, torture, and murder, *Titus Andronicus* is a theatrical expression of human revenge. It portrays the Roman Empire's descent into darkness, and its chaotic ending explores the idea that human civilization can be destroyed from within. The cry of revenge transformed into barbarism is uttered by a Roman lord: "Let Rome herself be bane unto herself."[10] The accusation, however, is not limited to the Romans, of course, but applies to us as well.

When dealing with the concept of revenge, the question of how it enters our daily lives is much less important than the question of how it can be prevented. Revenge is not first and foremost a theoretical concept, but a practical problem. Under certain circumstances, every individual is capable of revenge against another human being. To be human is to have the potential to become an executioner. This is because human beings are fallible. All people fail at some point. In other words, no one is a pure victim. Perhaps this is because innocence is an ideal, not a real state of being. We are all guilty of our innocence—even innocent people have the tendency to separate others into the categories of "good" and "bad." Their indifference sometimes causes more pain and harm to other people and communities than when violence is practiced directly. Indifference can be best explained as the depersonalization of the other. As William Blake wrote, "None can see the man in the enemy ... I cannot love my enemy for my enemy is not man but beast and devil."[11] This dispassionate form of discrimination is often based on the most trivial difference between "us" and "them." Recognizing this situation makes it clear that the problem is how to avoid opposing "us" to "them" or—as we do very often in North America—talking about the "West" and the "Rest."

This is not to say that social and political prejudices or religious and cultural intolerances do not create real problems for dialogue among individuals and between cultures. However, most of the barbarities in the world are the result of a reductionist view of civilization and humanity. One can find the foundations of such a reductionism in the miniaturization of individuals to make them fit into ideological boxes. The unquestioning acceptance of religious or cultural classifications as the unique modes for representing the concepts of humanity and civilization can, of course, be both a source of belligerent distortion and a negation of the eventual features of human commonality.

For human solidarity to fulfill all its potential, it must take root in a world whose members—or at least a great number of them—share the same values. We have no choice but to learn more about each other if we seriously intend to protect our shared values. By doing so, we help create an era of responsible global politics where intercultural learning replaces global mass culture. If we can succeed, even if only to some extent, in making intercultural dialogue the ground of our practical politics, that in itself would be an excellent point of departure for safeguarding international peace. This is not only a matter of tolerant people coming to terms, but of people of divergent convictions finding a common idea of tolerance. If ever there was a moment to engage in dialogue, it is the present one.

Dialogue is not easy. It is even more difficult when the world has become a dangerous and precarious place where rich and powerful individuals—murderers and scoundrels—hate to see people finding unity despite their differences and disagreements. Dialogue demands another spirit and another form of struggle, not one that celebrates military power or political violence, not one that cruelly hangs teenagers and imprisons intellectuals and artists, and not one that is Islamophobic or anti-Semitic, but a spirit and form of struggle that celebrates strength in debate and transparency in dialogue and embraces humility, thoughtfulness, and sincerity.

In the post-9/11 era, Muslims worldwide face discrimination and hatred due to the actions of minority extremist groups. As a result, Islamophobia has led to a widespread fear of Islam and Muslims. Islamophobia can be defined as more than a form of fear and hatred: it is also as a vengeful attitude against members of Islamic religion and culture. Among the stereotypes and misconceptions that are part of Islamophobia in the West is the belief that Muslims do not share common values with other religions and cultures. Muslims are portrayed as civilizational misfits with a violent political ideology. These perceptions are widely inaccurate and contribute toward the further stereotyping and polarization of Muslims. In reaction to events such as 9/11, the 2005 London bombings, the *Charlie Hebdo* killings, and the Paris attacks of November 13, 2015, people around the globe, but especially in the West, have developed a very harsh and negative stance toward Muslims worldwide. The reality is that the individuals responsible for global bloodshed, massacre, and terrorism are very often aliens within the Islamic community and openly declare themselves to be separate from the main body of Muslims. Nevertheless, the outrageous murder of innocent citizens in France by militant Muslims left people around the world, including the vast majority of followers of Islam, with a number of questions. Among them, the most fundamental from the non-Muslims is whether Islam is incompatible with free thought. Let us not hide behind the convenient general opinion that Islam is a religion of violence and the only way to save the West is to put extreme pressure on Muslims living in Europe and North America to abandon Islam. This path does not lead to any solution and is merely another form of intolerance and barbarity.

Islam, like Janus, has two faces. There is the tolerant, peaceful face, and there is the intolerant, violent face. That there is more than one face of Islam is unavoidable (as in any religion), especially at a time when huge transformations occur on an unprecedented global scale. There was a time when Muslim philosophers and theologians felt that if Muslims were eager to solve problems, they should return to the Qur'an and the Sunnah. This approach is no doubt good, but it has its problems. Returning to the Qur'an and the Sunnah is not easy and does not guarantee that all radical Islamists will end their violence and their monolithic interpretation of religious texts. The central question addressed to Islamists in particular, and to the Muslim world in general, is how to come to terms with their own civilizing process.

Being a Muslim is a lived experience. Islamic terrorism, or Islamism, is a radical mode of de-civilization, even though its actors claim that they are the closest to true Islamic civilization. In destroying the troublesome symbols of free thinking, the radical actors of the Muslim world are destroying their own cultural vitality and dynamism. Their Islamist culture of death has resulted in a death of Islamic culture. Radical Muslims have intensified the unresolved tension between Islamism and Islamic civilization. As a result, Muslims who argue for a civilizational Islam as opposed to an ideological Islam are seemingly expelled from the arena on the charge that they are not "Muslim enough." Voices within the Muslim community that insist that Islam should have nothing to do with hatred, terrorism, and mass murder find themselves marginalized. The representatives of a civilizational Islam do not seem to be confident enough to raise their voices or to step out of the comfort of their ivory towers and into Muslim public spheres.

Today, the vulnerabilities of Muslims around the world are such that radical and violent slogans are far more evocative than moderate and nonviolent ones. If Muslims want to continue to turn to Islam as a source of personal and communal identity and moral guidance, they need to move beyond the constant blame game. They must seek instead to revitalize elements of Islamic philosophy, science, and art in a new dialogical partnership with members of other spiritual traditions—and with the actual conditions that surround us in today's world. The language of hatred and violence in the Muslim community needs to be replaced by a "heart and mind" engagement and cooperation among Muslims and with other cultures. The urgent task for Islamic pluralists is to lift the shadow of violence from Islamic culture and recall Muslims to their traditions as an empathetic civilization that feels the sorrow of others and does not need an enemy to sustain itself. In doing this, they will strengthen cross-cultural goodwill to fight the dangerous rise of Islamophobia in Europe and North America and shape awareness in the Muslim community of the historical figures of nonviolence in Islam. This is not to say that Islamist extremism is not an issue for peace and dialogue among different cultures in today's world. However, most of the cruelties in the world, including those against Muslims, are committed in the name of a reductionist view of humanity. This process of degradation and reduction is founded on the presumption that to be a human being means to belong to a religious division such as Christianity, Islam, Hinduism, Judaism, or Buddhism.

The unquestioning acceptance of religious or cultural identities as the unique guarantors of the concepts of humanity and civilization can be both a source of belligerent distortion and a negation of the essential features of human commonality. There can be no human solidarity without mutual respect and mutual commitment among human beings. It is often the search for negotiation, where each side makes concessions to the other, that paves the way to managing social, political, and cultural tensions in our world. Neither Islamist extremism nor Islamophobia are modes of negotiation and acceptance of the other. Empathy and negotiation, unlike revenge and resentment, are ways to live next to the other and to renounce violence against the other. Cultures of intolerance allow virtually no room for dialogue because dialogue implies two partners who are equally free to assert what they think to be true and right.

The relevant question is not what we should believe, but what we should do about our beliefs. Answering this question was the task accomplished by great historical figures such as Mohandas Gandhi, Martin Luther King, Jr., and Abdul Ghaffar Khan. Abdul Ghaffar Khan was a Pashtun independence activist against the rule of the British Raj. His profound belief in the truth and effectiveness of nonviolence came from the depths of his personal experience of his Muslim faith. He said, "You see that the world is going toward destruction and violence. And the specialty of violence is to create hatred among people and to create fear. I am a believer in non-violence and I say that no peace or tranquility will descend upon the people of the world until non-violence is practiced, because non-violence is love and it stirs courage in people."[12] The legacy of tolerant Muslims like Abdul Ghaffar Khan may be of help in the task of overcoming clashes of ignorance and intolerance between Islam and the West.

5

To ignore evil is to become an accomplice to it.

MARTIN LUTHER KING, JR.[1]

IT IS REVEALING THAT IN A WORLD WHERE THERE is a high degree of vengefulness and resentment expressed in activities such as terrorism, fanaticism, and neo-colonialism, history can still be made by our choices. We live in a world of "overlapping destinies" where the fates of cultures are heavily intertwined. It is no longer a world of closed communities where tyrannical orders or religious traditions represent the sole source of historical legitimacy. According to the French-Bulgarian philosopher Tzvetan Todorov, "it is up to us, to those of us who live peaceful lives unbeset by the troubles of the world, to recognize and acknowledge these acts of dignity, caring, and creativity, to confirm their value and encourage them more than we habitually do."[2] These deeds, performed in extreme circumstances, shall act as a model for our "ordinary moral values and virtues," founding them on the "recognition that it is as easy to do good as to do evil."[3] It may help us understand human affairs to realize that history is neither fundamentally good nor fundamentally evil: it is a continuous effort to live even in the most unlivable circumstances. It is in this effort that the ethical is found in our century. It is the way for men and women to maintain their own humanity and responsibility toward the other in times of despair and discouragement. When there is a collective climate of self-deception and docile effortlessness, those who choose the ethical way are those who, first and foremost, manage to think freely and critically and have the strength of mind to question their own consciences, disputing the conformism and the rules in force around them. Dissent benefits others, while conformism benefits only oneself. Much of the time, one needs to follow one's inner voice to remain ethical. Those who conform do not serve the general interest of humanity. Small gestures in defence of forgiveness and human dignity take on a special value in today's contexts of revenge and cruelty. If we have to move in the direction of forgiveness and human dignity, we need to cultivate a deep humanistic commitment in the face of vengeful violence. We need, first and foremost, to rediscover our capacity to think and act ethically in a world that has become incapable of thinking or articulating anything other than what it has been conditioned to believe. This reminds me of what Solzhenitsyn said about Soviet ideology:

> Violence does not always necessarily take you physically by the throat and strangle you! More often it merely demands of its subjects that they declare allegiance to the lie, become accomplices in the lie. And the simple step of a simple, courageous man is not to take part in the lie, not to support deceit. Let the lie come into the world, even dominate the world, but not through me.[4]

What Solzhenitsyn described as a violent lie has become an even greater violence. What once remained a fantasy or a dream has become a big lie. We might think that resentment is now a matter of the past, but if we pause to ask ourselves which concept best describes our contemporary world, we need to consider Nietzsche's words in *On the Genealogy of Morals*: "Picture 'the enemy' as the man of *ressentiment* conceives him—and here precisely is his deed, his creation: he has conceived 'the evil enemy,' *'the Evil One,'* and this in fact is his basic concept, from which he then evolves, as an afterthought and pendant, a 'good one'—himself!"[5]

Should we take Nietzsche seriously? Nietzsche invites us to reflect on what he calls *ressentiment* because there is no German word for it. The French word *ressentiment* is very close in meaning to the English word "resentment." For Nietzsche, *ressentiment* becomes a philosophical concept. This definition is distinct from that used by Nietzsche's predecessors, who wrote about *ressentiment* as a sentiment of injustice and humiliation that translates into a wound and a pain; take for example the famous citation by Camille in Corneille's *Horace*, act IV, scene 5: "Rome, th' only object of my sad resentment! Rome, unto whom thine arm hath sacrific'd my Lover! Rome, that gave thee birth, and whom thou dost adore! Lastly, Rome that I hate because she honours thee!"[6] Nietzsche describes a man of *ressentiment* as the person who "is neither upright nor naïve, nor honest and direct with himself. His soul squints. His spirit loves hiding places, secret paths, and back doors. Everything furtive attracts him as his world, his security, his refreshment. He understands about remaining silent, not forgetting, waiting, temporarily diminishing himself, humiliating himself."[7] Nietzsche considers "resentment" to be the morality of slaves and opposes it to the morality of noble men, a master morality. The noble man is distinguished by a degree of self-respect, while the slave or the man of resentment is recognizable by his reactive attitude. According to Nietzsche, the slave comes to see his oppressive master as "evil" and uses the concept of "good" to describe himself in opposition to this master. This is exactly the opposite of what characterizes the noble man, who "conceives of the basic idea 'good' by himself, in advance and spontaneously, and only then creates a notion of 'bad'!"[8]

Nietzsche's man of resentment "knows all about keeping quiet, not forgetting, waiting, temporarily humbling and abasing himself."[9] This is a form of self-frustration that is completed by an act of resentment and revenge. In other words, men of resentment, guided by their "hatred of impotence," declare that "only those who suffer are good, only the poor, the powerless, the lowly are good; the suffering, the deprived, the sick, the ugly, are the only pious people, the only ones saved, salvation is for them alone, whereas you right, the noble and powerful, you are eternally wicked, cruel, lustful, insatiate, godless, you will also be eternally wretched, cursed and damned!"[10] Such an attitude is possible only if there is a "radical revaluation of their [enemies' and conquerors'] values, that is, through an act of the most deliberate revenge."[11] Nietzsche considers *ressentiment* to be a form of vengefulness based on envy and impotence. The repressed and frustrated feelings of the oppressed legitimize their reaction against the oppressor as the dominant enemy. For Nietzsche, this *ressentiment* is a commitment to revenge that seems to go beyond the tyrannies of the past. Aristotle held that tyranny, like other defective regimes, was characterized by the ruler's acting in his own interest rather than for the common good. However, with resentment, we are dealing with a mentality that requires a more extensive apparatus of repression precisely because it needs to destroy its supposed enemies.

We can find a mentality such as the one described by Nietzsche in the secular and religious political ideologies of the twentieth and twenty-first centuries. One of the most striking methods of political ideologies, either liberal or illiberal, is to create "enemies." This need to create enemies is what George Orwell called "a way of attaining salvation without altering one's conduct."[12] Since the enemy is always wrong, using violence against him is morally and politically approvable and legitimate. Here we have a difference between a conventional form of enmity, which might occur in everyday life, and a totalitarian enmity that, according to Hannah Arendt, opens the abyss of mass extermination. For Arendt,

> the fundamental difference between modern
> dictatorships and all other tyrannies of the past
> is that terror is no longer used as a means to
> exterminate and frighten opponents, but as an
> instrument to rule masses of people who are

perfectly obedient. Terror as we know it today strikes without any preliminary provocation, its victims are innocent even from the point of view of the persecutor.[13]

At the foundation of a totalitarian enmity is the concept of "totalitarian revenge," which is different in many ways from the "tyrannical revenge" that we encounter in Shakespearean tragedies such as *Macbeth* and *Titus Andronicus*. Totalitarian revenge starts where tyrannical forms of revenge stop. As such, totalitarian revenge "turns not only against its enemies but against its friends and supporters as well."[14] In the last chapter of her magnum opus on totalitarianism, Arendt describes in her own terms the essence of totalitarian revenge in the form of terror:

> Terror is the realization of the law of movement; its chief aim is to make it possible for the force of nature or of history to race freely through mankind, unhindered by any spontaneous human action. As such, terror seeks to "stabilize" men in order to liberate the forces of nature or history. It is this movement which singles out the foes of mankind against whom terror is let loose, and no free action of either opposition or sympathy can be permitted to interfere with the

elimination of the "objective enemy" of History
or Nature, or of the class or the race. Guilt and
innocence become senseless notions; "guilty"
is he who stands in the way of the natural or
historical process which has passed judgment
over "inferior races," over individuals "unfit to
live," over "dying classes and decadent peoples."
Terror executes these judgments, and before its
court, all concerned are subjectively innocent:
the murdered because they did nothing against
the system, and the murderers because they do
not really murder but execute a death sentence
pronounced by some higher tribunal.[15]

The creation of secular religions and the ideologiza-
tion of religion in the past one hundred years showed
us that we are dealing with new forms of resentful and
vengeful sentiments. The grand schemes of methodical
mass killing in the Stalinist Gulags and Nazi concentration camps were later continued in other forms of genocide and ethnic cleansing in Cambodia, Rwanda, and the
former Yugoslavia, to name only a few examples. In all
these cases, there was no explanation for the revenge and
resentment. Here, Arendt draws our attention to the fact
that the "concept of enmity is replaced by that of conspiracy, and this produces a mentality in which reality—real

enmity or real friendship—is no longer experienced and understood in its own terms but is automatically assumed to signify something else."[16]

This is roughly the experience I had as a political prisoner in Iran in 2006. I was not targeted as an enemy of the Iranian state but as a spy and a conspirator who was preparing a velvet revolution in Iran. Who's afraid of the "velvet revolution"? Those who understand neither Gandhian nonviolence nor the Eastern European velvet revolution. Perhaps this is why my absurd arrest and imprisonment seemed to have been taken from the Soviet playbook. As my mentor Cornelius Castoriadis used to say, the Union of the Soviet Socialist Republics was "four words, four lies."[17] Russia was an imperial state, not a union, it was never a Socialist system, and the Soviets were not democratically elected. However, the Soviet model of political rule and socio-economic relations dominated the perspective of the parties of the Left for the greater part of the twentieth century. The revenge taken by the Soviet bureaucracy under its new form of ideological oppression was supported by the theoretical tenets of Marxist-Leninism.

No novel better exposes the concept of revenge in the Soviet system than *The Confession* by Artur London.[18] The book is based on the true story of Czechoslovak Communist Artur London, a defendant in the 1952 trial for anti-state conspiracy centred around Rudolf Slánský. On

November 20, 1952, Rudolf Slánský, general secretary of the Communist Party of Czechoslovakia, and thirteen other leading party members, eleven of them Jews, were accused of participating in a Trotskyite-Titoite-Zionist conspiracy, and convicted. London, the deputy minister of foreign affairs at the time, was among the three who were sentenced to life imprisonment. Slánský and eleven others were hanged in Prague on December 3, 1952. In *The Confession*, upon which Costa-Gavras's film of the same title is based, London describes human vulnerability in the face of cruelty and shows us that during the ordeal of a prisoner in a totalitarian state, many facets of the prisoner's personality emerge. I see many similarities between Artur London's case and mine, with interrogators promising the defendants that if they confess, their lives will be spared. London describes the details of his confessions in a second book entitled *On Trial*:

> The day before the prosecutor's indictment Kohoutek brought me a pencil and paper and asked me to write out my last statement before the verdict. "You must stick to the line taken in your 'confessions' and prove to the party that you are continuing to do what is expected of you." A little later I gave him my draft. He left to see his "chiefs." Very early the next morning he returned

and gave me the corrected text. Three sentences had been crossed out and others had been added. He accused me of not having thought about it enough. "And now learn it by heart. And don't change anything. Otherwise you'll regret it." ... I still felt that my personality was split; I was both actor and spectator in this trial. One thought obsessed me: "So that was what happened at the trials of Moscow, Budapest, and Sofia. How could I and so many other communists, so many honest people, believe in them?"[19]

What London fails to add is that Nazism and Stalinism triumphed over liberal ideas in the first half of the twentieth century because they knew how to persuade the masses through lies. Moreover, their totalitarian character authorized the use of terror and lies, not through a process of consent but through the straightjacket of suspicion. What these ideologies needed to achieve their historical revenge were not only falling heads but signed confessions. By stripping away human judgment as the axis of history, totalitarian ideologies changed the focus to the individual's sense of revenge rather than to the system's insanity. The abuse of power was expressed through the promise of survival to those who renounced everything else. But this renunciation was a form of dehumanization.

The self-confession of guilt by the dehumanized prisoners suggested that their rational ability to judge political reality had been damaged, and displayed their forced desire to accept the Party's past crimes as their own. We see here ideological revenge projected onto sacrificial scapegoats who are judged in the name of the people. "Why me?" ask Artur London and other victims of Stalinism upon whom the Stalinist secret police and militias suddenly and inexplicably vented their revenge and resentment.

This question is also asked by Johann Moritz, the main protagonist of Constantin Virgil Gheorghiu's *The Twenty-Fifth Hour*, where the brutal revenge of Nazis and Stalinists against an ordinary man is described with profound intensity. However, there is much more to the book. As Gabriel Marcel, a French Christian existentialist, wrote in the preface to the French edition, "*The Twenty-Fifth Hour* is about a degraded form of life, a life which everything is turning against the real life, in other words, against creation and against love."[20] Gheorghiu shows in his novel that resentment is everywhere identical. His main character is first declared to be a Jew and taken to a camp; when the camp is liberated, he is declared to be a member of the "Master Race" and treated as an enemy by the Allies—all without the slightest regard for his humanity. "In 1938 I was in a Jewish camp in Rumania," says Johann in the last lines of the novel:

In 1940 in a Rumanian concentration camp in Hungary. In 1941 in a camp in Germany ... In 1945 in an American camp ... The day before yesterday I was released from Dachau. Thirteen years of camps. ... Tears welled up in his eyes. Now that he had been ordered to smile he could not bear it any longer. He felt he was going to burst into hysterical sobs like a woman, from sheer despair. This was the end. He could not go on. No living man could have gone on.[21]

The tragedy of Johann Moritz is that of all men and women who suffer from the evils of revenge. The revenge theme develops slowly in the mind of tragic literary characters. Moreover, some male and female protagonists of classical novels have no vengeful tendencies until they are inspired or forced to them by the sufferings and events that they have witnessed. *The Count of Monte Cristo* by Alexandre Dumas is probably one of the most remarkable revenge stories in modern literature. Its plot was inspired by an anecdote from real police files, which Jacques Peuchet, a French police archivist, wrote about under the title *The Diamond and the Vengeance*. It tells the story of a poor shoemaker, Picaud, who lived in Nîmes in 1807. Married to a rich woman, Picaud was falsely accused by three friends of being a spy for England and sent to the

Fenestrelle Fort, where he served as a servant to a rich Italian ecclesiastic. When the cleric died, he left his fortune to Picaud, who began plotting his revenge on the three men responsible for his arrest.[22]

The Count of Monte Cristo begins here, but Dumas divided his novel into three sections, which take place in Marseille, Rome, and Paris. The third part, in which Monte Cristo's revenge is accomplished, takes up 79 chapters of the book. Dumas's realist description of the sentiment and act of revenge goes further than characters, places, and events to reveal its basis in the complexity of human nature. Unlike Greek tragedies or Shakespearean plays, where revenge is situated in a larger context, revenge in *The Count of Monte Cristo* has an independent place. It has a value in and of itself and a symbolism of its own. In the words of F. W. J. Hemmings, one of the most respected literary scholars and specialists of French literature in the English-speaking world, "*Le Comte de Monte-Cristo*, a work that has a strong claim to be reckoned Dumas's masterpiece, is no doubt the greatest 'revenger's tragedy' in the whole history of novel. Yet it was written not by some aggrieved victim of society forever brooding over his wrongs, but on the contrary by the most blithely forgiving of men, who, though he could use a sharp tongue on occasion, never bore a grudge and never admitted to having enemies."[23] Monte Cristo is portrayed as a man who is alone with his exhausting and antinomian passions and can never regain peace and love. There remains, however, a hint of ambiguity in his grand design of revenge. "I wish to be Providence myself," says Monte Cristo, "for I feel that the most beautiful, noblest, most sublime thing in the world is to recompense and punish."[24] Monte Cristo sees himself as the hand of the Providence and repeats the words of God, "Vengeance is mine." But Dumas sees an end to the process of Monte Cristo's poisonous revenge in his pilgrimage into his past at Chateau d'If, where he spent ten or more years of his youth. The fortress is no longer a prison, as Monte Cristo is no longer Edmond Dantes. Freed from his desire for revenge, Dantes-Monte Cristo seeks to overcome and surpass resentment and madness.

Although Dumas takes his readers through the internal metamorphosis of an individual, *The Count of Monte Cristo* is more than a simple psychological novel. For Dumas, the ecstasy of revenge becomes a phenomenological odyssey, or perhaps what we can call a *Bildungsroman* of revenge that follows the progression of its protagonist's sufferings and sentiments. It is a narrative of self-education and a development in vengeance that traces the mutations and vicissitudes of a wounded and suffering consciousness. Dumas shows us a lust for revenge and rage for power at a time when Europe was entering a new epoch of its political history. In his novel, through Monte Cristo's odyssey of revenge, we can see a dialectical movement in the relationship between nation-state and national subject in nineteenth-century France. Umberto Eco sees the novel as essentially the proposition "What would 19th century France have been like if someone named the Count of Monte Cristo had lived there?"[25] The usual reply to Eco's question is to say that Dumas's special attention to the theme of revenge in *The Count of Monte Cristo* allows him to balance the psychology of human passion with politics, urban geography, bourgeois relations, and daily customs in nineteenth-century France. Finding such a balance is a rule in writing a historical novel, and yet a writer like Dumas is ready to break that rule in order to elaborate a revenge masterpiece. However, Dumas's novel is not merely a collection of vengeful actions by Dantes-Monte Cristo: it is the tale of archetypal vengeance by a man unjustly imprisoned who dreams about punishing the men who failed him. For Antonio Gramsci, the central revenge plot in *The Count of Monte Cristo* becomes "a real way of day-dreaming."[26] However, if one doesn't want to be as dismissive as Gramsci is of Dumas's novel, the revenge of Monte Cristo can be understood in the mirror of Edmond Dantes' process of waiting and hoping, displayed when he writes in a letter: "until the day when God deigns to reveal the future to man, all human wisdom is contained in these two words—'Wait and hope.'"[27]

Like Monte Cristo, Ahab, the ship captain of Herman Melville's *Moby-Dick*, is also plagued by the desire for revenge. *Moby-Dick* is a modern epic that takes the form of a story of colossal revenge, the revenge of a man against a white whale. However, this whale is outside the knowledge of whalers, because it is the object of Captain Ahab's revenge. If we omit the white whale (understood this way) from the story, *Moby-Dick* becomes an insignificant tale of a whaling voyage. What makes Melville's novel, in the words of Jean-Paul Sartre, an "imposing monument"[28] is the description of the Promethean battle of Captain Ahab against a mythological animal of the seas. The white whale's resemblance to a beast-God turns Ahab into an agent of ritual, of mythological vengeance. As passionate readers of *Moby-Dick*, we cannot miss the substantial tie that Melville establishes between Ahab and the white whale. It is the instinct of revenge that creates this deep affinity between the hunting priest and the hunted icon. The man and the animal share the same fundamental destiny, which links them in a Hegelian struggle for recognition. As close as Melville gets to a phenomenological voyage of self-discovery, the ultimate truth of the experience of revenge of the hunter against the hunted is in Ahab's farewell to his ship. He says, "Oh, lonely death on lonely life! Oh, now I feel my topmost greatness lies in my topmost grief."[29] Though Melville did not further dramatize the words of his tragic hero, he shows us Ahab going down with no triumph or joy. The revenge that drives Ahab, as Melville perceives, is as much and as natural a part of the human passion as its mate, the spirit of cosmic fury. Melville's exploration of the monomaniacal revenge that drives Captain Ahab to his death is balanced in the novel with an epistemological quest for truth. Since the "mystic-marked whale" is unknowable, it "must remain unpainted to the last."[30]

Melville spells out this human fallibility in his understanding of the Leviathan:

> So there is no earthly way of finding out precisely what the whale really looks like. And the only mode in which you can derive even a tolerable idea of his living contour, is by going a whaling yourself; but by so doing, you run no small risk of being eternally stove and sunk by him. Wherefore, it seems to me you had best not be too fastidious in your curiosity touching this Leviathan.[31]

Melville's elaboration of Captain Ahab's revenge must be seen in relation to the theological context that endows the entire story with Biblical significance. In his madness, Ahab imitates the God-Absolute. He interprets the whale's attack against him and his ship as divine will.

In confronting the beast, "his soul must be made monstrous,"[32] as the French poet Arthur Rimbaud is held to have said twenty years after *Moby-Dick* was first published. In his pain and delirium, Ahab resembles Macbeth, who is haunted by the prophecy of the three witches. Ahab is locked in his nightmarish imagination. He stops thinking about revenge and only feels revenge. "Ahab never thinks," writes Melville in the last chapter of his book, "he only feels, feels, feels, that's tingling enough for mortal man!"[33] One ought to reflect on the labyrinth-shaped universe of *Moby-Dick*. Lewis Mumford describes Melville's novel as the "presentation of the demonic dark side of man, today so visible." But he also talks about it as "a parable on the mystery of evil and the accidental malice of the universe."[34] In the end, Ahab goes down with his ship, along with his hate and suffering. He faces his "lonely death on lonely life." Through his vengeance, he becomes one with the whale. In the madness of one who dares to confront God, Ahab's madness turns into an "audacious, immitigable, and supernatural revenge." With heroic boldness, he faces the white whale's destructive attack: "Towards thee I roll, thou all-destroying but unconquering whale; to the last I grapple with thee, from hell's heart I stab at thee; for hate's sake I spit my last breath at thee."[35]

When I read this last passage of Melville's novel, I realize that our century is still not prepared to understand

Moby-Dick as an ode to human revenge. What *Moby-Dick* teaches us is more than the tragedy of the revenge of a sea captain. It is the anatomy of the human soul in modern times. With Melville, revenge is not an abstract concept; it is a part of the world, but it requires a talionic return, given the victim's suffering. As the German phenomenologist Max Scheler suggests, "Revenge, envy, the impulse to detract, spite, *Schadenfreude*, and malice lead to *ressentiment* only if there occurs neither a moral self-conquest (such as *genuine* forgiveness in the case of revenge) nor an act of some other adequate expression of emotion (such as verbal abuse or shaking one's fist) and if this restraint is caused by a pronounced awareness of *impotence*."[36] Revenge is internalized as a reactive feeling and a lasting mental attitude that develops into a sense of powerlessness. This is what Gilles Deleuze states in his study of Nietzsche: "*Ressentiment* is the triumph of the weak as weak, the revolt of the slaves and their victory as slaves. In their victory, the slaves form a type ... The type of slave (reactive type) is defined by prodigious memory, by the power of *ressentiment*."[37] But if, as Nietzsche, Scheler, and Deleuze affirm, a vengeful victim of a cruelty is someone who will continue to resent his or her offender without acting, how can that victim address his or her sufferings and "reverse the irreversible"?[38]

6

The whole idea of compassion is based on a keen awareness of the interdependence of all these living beings,
which are all part of one another, and all involved in one
another.

THOMAS MERTON[1]

"TO SHUT OURSELVES UP IN BURNING SILENCE WILL
be our greatest punishment," Leonardo says in Federico
García Lorca's *Blood Wedding*. "And you think time heals
and walls cover up, and it's not true, it's not true. When
things reach their center, they can't be stopped!"[2] In these
words Lorca grasps the deepest secret of our hearts and
expresses it in drama. He knew that humans die and
nations fall, but poetry lives on. Lorca was brutally assas-
sinated at the hands of the fascist Falangists on August
19, 1936, four weeks after Franco's army rose against the
democratically elected Popular Front government. Lorca

fell victim to the hatred and revenge of those who refused to accept him as marginal, as committed to a way of life that called theirs into question. However, Lorca's assassins did not succeed in settling accounts or getting even, nor did they put the world of the mid-twentieth century back in balance. Their act of revenge brought them greater harm than Lorca, who became a hero of the Spanish Civil War and a martyr poet. How much does revenge satisfy the person who achieves it? Do agents of revenge suffer from their own wrongdoing, or do they achieve a sense of justice through their sentiment of vengeance and vindictiveness? Is revenge a justified punishment based on a morally correct insight, or is it, with its conception of *lex talionis* (an eye for an eye, a tooth for a tooth), a violation of human dignity? How can one overcome revenge without losing a sense of justice? It is not necessary to multiply such questions to understand that motives of revenge underlie most of the atrocities and horrors in history. If there is one lesson that the history of the past hundred years has shown us, it is that responding to one horror with another does not put an end to the suffering of individuals and nations. It is long past time to ask, what future comes out of revenge?

Let us have no misunderstanding. Revenge lurks behind the most normal of thoughts and actions, and in places and times where and when it is least expected. It is also evoked in a bitter vagueness full of distant memories. Revenge emerges, disappears, and emerges again. It is an unchallenged power with an unusual and mysterious perfume. The hatred and resentment of the vengeful remind us of the tragic nature of violence, an essential element of life. Life is a school of revenge and violence, as Euripides, Seneca, Shakespeare, Melville, Dostoyevsky, and many others teach us, but it is also a long road to forgiveness.

Forgiveness is not a philosophical system, though it has been thought about and elaborated on by philosophers. It is not a philosophy consciously worked out and conveyed in a logical and rational form. However, every great philosopher's work contains a conception of forgiveness, just as life contains an invisible essence denoting its distinction. All great philosophers have, in one way or another, tried to decipher some scent of the reality of forgiveness. Philosophy is always an act of forgiving through addressing all the things that surround individuals in life. The vision of life and humanity that shines in every work of philosophy is founded on the concept of forgiveness. Forgiveness is the mentor of life. It is exalted as an urge for existence. The forgiveness that each one of us has inside is the value of life, around which everything revolves. To deny forgiveness would be to deny an indispensable condition of our life. Philosophy is an expression of life, and forgiveness is the centre of gravity of philosophy. Philosophy is obsessed with the meaning of life as forgiveness. Philosophy gives us an awareness of forgiveness that intensifies our consciousness of life and our conception of existence that is fulfilled in the willingness to reach an understanding of eternity.

Every life is eternity. Forgiveness comes like a candle to light up our existence. It is like a fire in our hands that does not burn. It reveals the deepest secrets of our hearts. Forgiveness is a spiritual freedom from the chains of revenge. The human spirit can and does conquer revenge, as it conquers time and space. Through forgiveness, individuals leave the impression of spiritual grace on Earth. Forgiveness is not an idea, it is empathy. Empathy begins at the point where ideas end. We see in empathy the original substance that holds humanity together. Empathy is being with the other because of the otherness of the other. Forgiveness is the purification of a vengeful impulse. The function of forgiveness is to apprehend something outside our willful actions of revenge and violence. It is the only consolation that changes the anger and hatred of the vengeful into a new fountain of life.

It is curious and significant that we still find it difficult to see forgiveness clearly and to analyze it in detail, perhaps because we know that recognition of the necessity of forgiveness remains uncertain, an action that transcends the wounded and painful bounds of history. Forgiveness, however, is not an unapproachable destiny. It is like a good friend who knocks on our door at times of pain and sorrow. There is a poem by Federico García Lorca that expresses this feeling: "My heart I offer you. A heart that's human."[3] Revenge, resentment, and vengeance fall drop by drop on our heart until, in despair, wisdom comes through the grace of forgiveness. The idea of redeeming an individual, a nation, or the whole Earth through forgiveness is an old dream, also expressed in Alfred, Lord Tennyson's *Ulysses*: "The lights begin to twinkle from the rocks / The long day wanes / the low moon climbs / the deep moans round with many voices. / Come, my friends, 'Tis not too late to seek a newer world."[4]

Building a "newer world" is implicit in Hannah Arendt's belief in the human capacity to bring forth a new beginning. This new beginning is related to the human capacity to act and to be free. Politics, argues Arendt, is the realm where human beings act in concert. In other words, "action, though it may be started ... by single individuals for very different motives, can be accomplished only by some joint effort, in which the motivation of single individuals ... no longer counts."[5] Something similar is true for the conditions of the irreversibility and unpredictability of public action. However, according to Arendt, the two concepts of forgiveness and promise can remedy and correct these two dimensions of human action. In Arendt's brief discussion of the two concepts, promising responds to the unpredictability of action, whereas forgiveness responds to its irreversibility: "The possible redemption from the predicament of irreversibility—of being unable to undo what one has done though one did not, and could not, have known what he was doing—is the faculty of forgiving."[6] For Arendt, only the possibility of forgiveness saves future actions from utter desolation and degradation: "Without being forgiven, released from the consequences of what we have done, our capacity to act would, as it were, be confined to one single deed from which we could never recover; we would remain the victims of its consequences forever, not unlike the sorcerer's apprentice who lacked the magic formula to break the spell."[7] The notion of undoing what has been done suggests to Arendt the Christian notion of forgiveness. She tracks the social and political origins of the concept of forgiveness to Jesus of Nazareth. According to Arendt, Jesus uses the language of forgiveness when he asks God to forgive his murderers—"for they know not what they do."[8] The moment of violence against Christ explains and exemplifies clearly the redemptive content and context of forgiveness. By forgiving sins on Earth, Jesus hints at his prophetic identity while establishing an eschatological bridge between the divine and the human. The declaration that "the Son of Man has authority on earth to forgive sins"[9] is a Christological statement concerning the intervention of Christ in the *res publica*. That is why, according to Arendt, Christ's act of forgiving is primarily a human act, because forgiveness is a human faculty, not a divine one: "Jesus maintains against the 'scribes and Pharisees' first that it is not true that only God has the power to forgive, and second that this power does not derive from God—as though God, not men, would forgive through the medium of human beings—but on the contrary must be mobilized by men toward each other before they can hope to be forgiven by God also."[10]

This notion of divine forgiveness does not imply a state of immutability. Rather, it points to the necessity of forgiveness as a possibility and an openness. The more difficult the state of immutability, the more the necessity of forgiveness. In a curious way, then, forgiveness sustains the community by breaking through to the new. In the Christian context, forgiveness is the transformation of the past, not its abolition, because the community must move forward and heal its past wounds. The death of Jesus, therefore, is understood as a sacrifice that consolidates the establishment of a covenant between God and the followers of Jesus. This is what we read in Mark 14:24: "And he said unto them, This is my blood of the new testament, which is shed for many."[11] That is why we see the phrase "for the forgiveness of sins,"[12] which implies atonement for sin, in the Gospel of Matthew.

However, the Christian view of forgiveness is not merely liberation or preservation of human beings from suffering, but a way out of the guilt in which humanity is implicated. From this perspective, we may begin to see the Christian invitation to forgiveness less in individual terms and more in a community context. Forgiveness appears in Christian faith as a response to what cannot be changed by humans and can be forgiven only by God. The death of Jesus is portrayed as an eschatological event in association with an act of remission that implies a violent death and a peace-offering. It is, then, implied that the spirit that Jesus exemplifies in his death on the cross is that of forgiveness. Here, as before, the suffering and the horror of the death of Jesus are consistent with his teachings and previous acts of forgiving, such as those found in the following passages:

> But that ye may know that the Son of man hath power on earth to forgive sins.[13]

> Verily I say unto you, All sins shall be forgiven unto the sons of men.[14]

Wherefore I say unto thee, Her sins, which are
many, are forgiven.[15]

For if you forgive men their trespasses, your
heavenly Father will also forgive you: But if you
forgive not men their trespasses, neither will your
Father forgive your trespasses.[16]

In all of these passages, reception of the favour of God,
forgiving the wrongs of others, and the love of Christ
appear as the three-fold condition of forgiveness. However, as in the passage from Matthew 6:14, any attitude
of rejection of forgiveness, meaning a hostility toward
the Spirit of God, is unforgivable. Therefore, he alone is
forgiven who is received into divine approval. According to the model of Christ on the cross, forgiveness represents the possibility of change and transformation for
individuals and for nations. Forgiveness is, therefore, a
precondition for reconciliation. Forgiveness and reconciliation are concepts that are accepted and practiced by all
religious traditions. In some religions, such as Buddhism,
forgiveness is necessary in order to end the suffering of
both victims and wrong-doers. As the *Jātakamālā*, one of
the greatest masterpieces of Sanskrit literature, argues,
"It is other people's suffering which makes people suffer: it is that which they cannot endure, not their own

suffering."[17] Most religious traditions define forgiveness as an interpersonal transformation. When someone forgives a wrongdoer, it is the forgiver who changes. In this sense, forgiveness is a two-way street that offers a positive model for caring and empathy without necessarily absolving the wrongdoer of all responsibility for what he or she has done. If forgiveness happens, it happens as a result of confrontation with old wounds. These wounds are not forgotten, but they can and must be healed. The past lives with its wounds; the future does not. History is more than a realm of wounds and frustrations, of self-interest and self-preservation: it is the sphere of actualization of human compassion. Each nation finds in history its own way of realizing compassionate instincts.

Acts of forgiveness are rare in Greek tragedies. Forgiveness is not a virtue in Homer's world as it is in our modern, post-Christian world. There is substantial Homeric evidence that in his world overcoming anger is distinct from forgiving and abandoning the desire for revenge. Just before killing Hector, Achilles addresses the Trojan hero in these terms:

> Hector, talk not to me, curse you, of covenants.
> As between lions and men there are no oaths
> of faith, nor do wolves and lambs have hearts of
> concord but plan evils continually one against

the other, so is it not possible for you and me to be friends, nor will there be oaths between us till one or the other has fallen, and glutted with his blood Ares, the warrior with tough shield of hide. Take thought of all manner of valor: now you must be a spearman and a bold warrior. No more is there any escape for you, but soon will Pallas Athene vanquish you by my spear. Now will you pay back the full price of all my sorrows for my comrades whom you slew when you raged with your spear.[18]

Achilles kills Hector, but he pities Priam, Hector's father and the ruler of Troy, who departs in the night with his son's corpse, and the great Homeric epic ends with the burial of Hector. Pity is no doubt a form of healing, but it is not an act of forgiving. What Achilles does for Priam is emotionally powerful, but it does not generate compromise and reconciliation. To practice forgiveness is to supersede revenge. In other words, the logic of forgiveness is woven by the interdependence of the offender and the victim. This relationship exists even beyond the religious attitudes of forgiveness, which include forms of liberation from the contamination of sins and the weight of fate.

Moreover, the willingness to forgive indicates concern for the sufferings of the forgiver and the conscience of the person forgiven, and attention to the welfare of the community. Maimonides, the Jewish philosopher of Cordoba, puts this point in perspective: "The Law as a whole aims at two things: the welfare of the soul and the welfare of the body ... The latter aim consists in the governance of the city and the well-being of the states of all its people according to their capacity."[19] What is crucial to the notion of forgiveness and social and political relations among human beings is neither the Christian promise of God's forgiveness, nor Aristotle's discussion of the ways of opposing another person's anger, but patterns of living in harmony with others.

As hopeful as this message of the need to live together may be, it is confronted by the massive challenges and horrors of the twentieth century, such as the Holocaust, the Gulag, the killing fields of Pol Pot, or the ethnic cleansing in the former Yugoslavia. These terrifying human sufferings leave a strong sense of bitterness for the destiny of humanity. However, in all these cases of horror, the disgust and nausea they evoke is accompanied by an ethical awareness beyond revenge. Assuredly, not all survivors of the Nazi concentration camps or victims of the Stalinist Gulags consider forgiveness to be a way to exit their nightmares and sufferings. For Vladimir Jankélévitch, a French philosopher born to a Russian Jewish family, who was profoundly marked by the experience of the survivors of the Nazi camps, the key issue was the tension between the moral imperative of unconditional forgiveness and the unforgivable experience of Nazi crimes:

> To pardon! But who ever asked us for a pardon? It is only the distress and the dereliction of the guilty that would make a pardon sensible and right. When the guilty are fat, well nourished, prosperous, enriched by the "economic miracle," a pardon is a sinister joke. No, a pardon is not suitable for the swine and their sows. Pardoning died in the death camps.[20]

In broad outline, Jankélévitch's writings speak against the common belief that "time heals all wounds" or "to understand all is to forgive all" (*tout comprendre, c'est tout pardonner*). Jankélévitch holds that forgiveness is not the result of the passage of time and that if an action can be "fully understood" there is no need to forgive it. Jankélévitch then points to the unlimited or what he calls the "imprescriptable" essence of crimes against humanity that prevail against any passing of time or human understanding. More than anything else, Jankélévitch wants to show us that forgiving is a challenging task that cannot be accomplished easily. Eagerness to forgive the Nazis, for instance, is unjustified. The troubling dilemma

Jankélévitch postulates is that "the debate between for-giveness and the unforgivable will never have an end. The moral dilemma that ensues is insoluble, for if the imperative of love is unconditional and does not have any restrictions, then the obligation to annihilate evil, and if not to hate it … at least to reject its negating force … is no less imperious than the duty to love."[21] Jankélévitch does not believe in the process of normalization of for-giveness. For him, not to pardon or to forgive is a way to save the memory of the Holocaust from oblivion: "Par-doning died in the death camps."[22]

In many ways, Jankélévitch, who fought with the French Resistance against the Nazis, was attempting to distinguish forgiveness morally and ontologically from the act of excusing wrongdoers and the process of heal-ing wounds. Distancing himself from the everydayness of our lives, Jankélévitch's account of forgiveness is purely apolitical, related instead to love and justice. He refuses to submit to the momentary call of the political sphere because he rejects the idea of failing the memory of past victims. Thus, according to him, we need to make a choice:

> Of all the values, love for humans is the most sacred, but indifference to crimes against human-ity … against the essence and humanity of the person, is the most sacrilegious of all misdeeds.

Either moral judgment will hesitate indefinitely ... or we will choose to forgive the miserable person, although it may mean the establishment of the reign of hangmen for one thousand years; or, in order that the future be saved and that essential values survive, we will agree to prefer violence and force without love over a love without force. Such was, as we know, the heroic choice of the Resistance ... It is better to disavow oneself in punishing than to contradict oneself in forgiving![23]

That said, Jankélévitch's philosophical treatment of forgiveness totally ignored the flow of time in political life. Unlike Arendt, who considered "redemption from irreversibility" to be the essence of the act of forgiving, Jankélévitch pointed to forgiving the inexcusable and incomprehensible as the proper goal of forgiveness: "When a crime can neither be justified, nor explained, nor even understood, when, with everything that could be explained having been explained ... when the atrocity has neither mitigating circumstances, nor excuses of any sort, and when the hope of a generation has to be abandoned, then there is no longer anything else to do but to forgive."[24] Forgiveness cannot forgive anything but the unforgivable; otherwise it will lose its meaning.

Jacques Derrida pointed to the same idea in his essay *On Cosmopolitanism and Forgiveness*. but added a point that is missing in the arguments of both Arendt and Jankélévitch: the loss of the human capacity to forgive. For Derrida, the right to forgive or not to forgive belongs to the victims, and therefore forgiveness should keep its "heterogeneous and irreducible" essence with regard to the political and the legal:

> What I dream of, what I try to think as the 'purity' of a forgiveness worthy of its name, would be a forgiveness without power: unconditional but without sovereignty. The most difficult task, at once necessary and apparently impossible, would be to dissociate unconditionality and sovereignty. Will that be done one day? It is not around the corner, as is said. But since the hypothesis of this unpresentable task announces itself, be it as a dream for thought, this madness is perhaps not so mad.[25]

What we are left with, then, is the tension between the possibility offered by the human capacity to forgive and the ethical moment of forgiveness in life. In other words, if forgetfulness is an insult to the memory of those who suffered, rejecting the human capacity for forgiveness shuts the door to empathic repair on the transcendence of vengefulness. Once revenge is arrested by the rise of the ethical, consciousness of the miseries and sufferings of victims will replace the previous horror and violence.

7

I truly believe that compassion provides the basis of human survival, the real value of human life.

THE DALAI LAMA[1]

MAX STIRNER ONCE ARGUED, "I HAVE BASED MY CASE on Nothing."[2] Though Stirner does not refer to it as such, this "nothing" can be interpreted as forgiveness,. It is the act of basing one's case on something that, while it appears to be groundless, is important; forgiveness is nothing, in the sense that it has no meaning in and of itself. Humans give meaning to forgiveness by endorsing it or by dismissing it. There are few earthly acts more meaningful than forgiveness, as forgiveness is worked out through human destiny. The philosophy of forgiveness is the expression of our destiny as social-historical beings. In this destiny of ours, necessity and choice act jointly. Choice is the outcome of necessity, and necessity forces an inevitable choice.

Forgiveness belongs to the realm of necessity, while giving meaning to forgiveness belongs to the realm of choice. It is because humans have a tragic destiny that they can give meaning to the act of forgiving. At first sight, nothing seems more contradictory, but if one looks at the matter from a deeper point of view, it is possible to understand why a philosopher like Nietzsche takes his stand under the banner of *amor fati* (love of fate).[3] At the same time, he holds that Man has a capacity for heroic suffering because Man is able to give meaning to Nothing and to transcend it. However, giving meaning to Nothing is like walking on the edge of an abyss—there is no guarantee of getting to the other side. Life undoubtedly contains a strong element of the tragic, although it might not be seen and felt by everyone. If this is so, where are we to find the strength to cross this abyss? Perhaps we can find it by looking clearly at the principle of life and accepting that the world is both a realm of fear, revenge, and death and a realm of care, love, and forgiveness. Life, the true life of human beings, is not biological, hedonistic, and appetitive, but spiritual and determined by consciousness. To be human is to be an animal that can transcend life through the tragic experience of becoming. The rise of what is new, of what has not been before, is the greatest aspect of this becoming.

Forgiveness, as a new beginning, is a constitutive element of this becoming. Forgiving as newness is a transcendent breakthrough in the mystery of life itself. Moreover, it is the result of a creative act that passes through the refining furnace of suffering. Forgiveness is found in the complexity of the process of living. It is the triumph of the life of spirit over the spirit of evil. Jacob Boehme, the German Christian mystic, is believed to have said "the love of God operates in the darkness, as a burning fire."[4] Forgiveness is like a light that operates in darkness. It confronts the suffering that life with others brings us. But suffering is not the only basic fact of human existence. Man is both a suffering creature and a forgiving being. To say, "I forgive, therefore I am" is a more resounding phrase , and a more justifiable cry in today's world of political chaos than Descarte's *cogito ergo sum* (I think, therefore I am).

In forgiving, humans experience creative jubilation and empathic exaltation. Here, everything turns on the experience of integrality and harmony. The struggle for the realization of integrality is a struggle against the source of suffering: the spirit of revenge. The vengeful ego is an ego that has not yet transcended itself. This is what Pascal underlines when he argues, "*le moi est haïssable*" (the egotistical self is hateful).[5] A state of forgiveness is the discovery of exchange and harmony as the antithesis of revenge and suffering. However, suffering is the sole cause of the rise of forgiveness. The capacity to suffer from evil gives meaning to something of greater depth: the power to forgive. Without suffering in life and encountering evil in history, there is no possibility for humans to give a transcendental meaning to life. If there was only evil, humans would be insane, but because we also have the capacity to break away from evil and from the suffering created by it, the intensity of forgiveness is linked to that of life itself. The affirmation of forgiveness is essential to the affirmation of life in general, not only one's own life. Only by taking the risk of forgiveness can one live authentically. No human being is so mad a creature that he or she cannot forgive; none is so mad that he or she can dismiss the capacity of forgiveness.

Dostoyevsky understood this philosophy better than anyone. According to him, compassion is the absolute moral imperative. He was the first novelist to fully dramatize the principle of compassion through a novelistic character. In *The Idiot*, Prince Myshkin is a Christ-like character who pursues his worldliness through goodness, humility, and compassion, but his saintly manners make him unfit for social life, and he is labeled an idiot. As a character who lives the truth of living life, Myshkin is a glimpse of Christ's forgiveness and compassionate love. For Dostoyevsky, the meaningfulness of life is closely related to the necessity of compassion. Myshkin's all-forgiving eye shares the same perspective as the compassionate empathy of Sonya in *Crime and Punishment*, who assures Raskolnikov that they will "bear the cross together," and the infinite mercifulness of Alyosha in *The Brothers Karamazov*. Dostoyevsky's latter example is poignant:

> Alyosha stood, gazed, and suddenly threw himself down on the earth. He did not know why he embraced it. He could not have told why he longed so irresistibly to kiss it, to kiss it all. But he kissed it weeping, sobbing, and watering it with his tears, and vowed passionately to love it, to love it forever and ever. "Water the earth with the tears of your joy and love those tears," echoed in his soul. What was he weeping over? Oh! in his rapture he was weeping even over those stars, which were shining to him from the abyss of space, and he was not ashamed of that ecstasy. There seemed to be threads from all those innumerable worlds of God, linking his soul to them, and it was trembling all over in contact with other worlds. He longed to forgive everyone for everything, and to beg forgiveness. Oh, not for himself, but for all men, for all and for everything.[6]

Alyosha's loving sentiments are neither self-centred nor proud. On the contrary, they are humble, pure, and wholeheartedly sincere. Dostoyevsky's message for our world is the ontological quality of this humility and sincerity. Only if forgiveness is conceived as a real experience of "living together" can this message be understood. This conception of forgiveness is given splendid expression by Dostoyevsky in the passage of *The Brothers Karamazov* where Ivan questions Alyosha on the terrifying atrocities perpetuated on innocent children:

> "Imagine that you are creating a fabric of human destiny with the object of making men happy in the end, giving them peace and rest at last, but that it was essential and inevitable to torture to death only one tiny creature—that little child beating its breast with its fist, for instance— and to found that edifice on its unavenged tears, would you consent to be the architect on those conditions? Tell me, and tell the truth." "No, I wouldn't consent," said Alyosha softly.[7]

Ivan's terrifying question about the tears of a little child poses the problem of evil in human nature. Dostoyevsky's central response to this question is "shared responsibility." In a certain respect, what we learn from reading

Dostoyevsky is that forgiveness is the art of developing a sense of coexistence. Dostoyevsky goes even further and famously claims that coexistence as a communal responsibility means "all are guilty for all."[8] This communion of human hearts can be considered a moral awareness that rests upon a beautiful experience of forgiving and being forgiven. This atmosphere of universal solidarity infuses a passion for truth with a moral imperative for empathy, both of which are missing in our contemporary world. This ontology of empathy, the concordance of hearts, is a way of living together that is dismissed by the quantifiable world of techno-scientific positivism. In the words of the French philosopher Paul Ricoeur, "If one day the heart could have been opposed to reason, it was not because it was irrational—according to Pascal, the heart even apprehends the first principles—but because it does not proceed by means of analysis and argument, rising as it does from the depth of life toward the absolute pole in a single movement."[9] To a significant degree, what our century has lost is "conscience," that is, "the law written on the heart." Conscience—the universal symbol of our humanity—has been betrayed. I am reminded of a memorable line uttered by the famous French actor Fernandel in one of the scenes of *La Loi, c'est la Loi*: "*La conscience, c'est comme une personne qu'on estime. Quand on la trompe une fois, on n'ose plus la regarder en face.*" (The conscience is like a person we admire. Once we deceive her, we do not dare to face her any longer.)[10] Perhaps the time has come for us to reassert the practice of questioning according to conscience as a revolt against the moral distortion of mankind.

Frankly speaking, the tragedy of today's world is that, unlike what Immanuel Kant thought, neither the starry heavens above nor the moral law within fill our minds. Perhaps it is for this reason that the masses consider the question of forgiveness to be only a naive and unsatisfactory response to the problem of revenge and cruelty. Some see a murderous God as an adequate response to moral crisis and the sufferings of humanity. They come to believe that killing innocent people pleases God. Others have killed God and naively accepted that the villainy and caprices of humanity can be explained by the new church of science and technology. In both cases, humankind is degraded and denigrated, not only in our moral impotence but in our lack of consciousness of this impotence. I am nostalgic for a world where living and dying were at some point adventures in human experience. It is not weakness to need to bow down to futility and insignificance.

History shows us that humans are frail and fragile, but history also shows us that Man's living reality is clothed with hope. No other century has ever faced such a challenge of embracing hope or abandoning it once for all;

no century has ever walked so precisely on the tightrope of history. In this century, it is our fate, yours and mine, to be guardians of a heritage we did not begin in a world we have turned into a nightmare. If our century is to grow in wisdom and in moral stature, we should think of forgiveness as unfinished business. We may not reach this goal for humanity today or tomorrow—we may not reach it in our lifetime—but the quest for forgiveness and an end to revenge is the greatest political adventure of our century. Whatever the future brings, our foremost aim should be to uphold and defend forgiveness as a solution to political evil.

8

Courageous people do not fear forgiving, for the sake of peace.

NELSON MANDELA[1]

GIVEN THESE GRIM TIMES, WHAT KIND OF FORGIVE-ness should we seek? Not the forgiveness of the slave or the promise of injustice. I am talking about genuine forgiveness, the kind of forgiveness that makes civic friendship worth practicing, the kind of forgiveness that enables individuals and nations to become more mature and to build a life of plurality and passion for future generations. Maturity, according to Immanuel Kant, is the ability to make use of one's own understanding and to emerge from one's "self-incurred immaturity."[2] Talking about true forgiveness requires a level of maturity that makes it possible to discern the worthy from the unworthy, because becoming a forgiving individual or creating a forgiving political system is not the result of will alone. Forgiveness is not the result of meeting one or two requirements: there is no such thing as a single and simple solution for forgiveness, nor is there a magic formula. Recognizing forgiveness as a process requires us to adopt an enlightened attitude that does not deny the value of our ethical capacities or discourage us in the name of a necessary rational end. Given this, there can be no doubt about one aspect of the agenda of forgiveness: political experiences in contemporary history have shown us that if we want to be masters, not victims, of our destinies, we cannot give way to blind prejudice or to the victory of might at the expense of right.

Many people around the world today don't really understand the meaning of rights. While tyranny is the most obvious and vivid demonstration of the failure of rights, the cause of human rights and individual dignity is still claimed to have ever-increasing momentum in today's world. But the right to forgiveness is an elemental requirement of human justice. The harsh realities of poverty and social injustice will not be solved merely by political promises. The task we need to set ourselves is to tear apart the fabric of lies and misconceptions in our so-called civilized world and replace them with a deep commitment to the core of forgiveness. Forgiveness is the eternal safeguard of liberty, and opposition to forgiveness is the surest road to hatred and violence. Every person is entitled to resist the act of forgiving, but no individual or nation that pledges to create freedom and justice can heal its wounds without a willingness to face the truth about its past evils. A nation with a moral commitment to forgiveness cannot afford to do less: "Except the Lord keep the city, the watchman waketh but in vain."[3]

In this century, forgiveness—by choice rather than by fate—is the safeguard of world peace. We should therefore ask how we can exercise this choice of ours with wisdom and responsibility. It is clear that an individual or a nation that forgives its past without turning its back on it and forgetting it has the courage to confront the hidden dangers of its own destiny, but courage alone is not enough. Courage is not necessarily the readiness to respond to challenges at any time, but rather the virtue of leading through learning. However, the advancement of learning depends on the power of listening: listening is a necessary component of forgiveness. As Archbishop Desmond Tutu pointed out during the Truth and Reconciliation Commission in South Africa,

> [Forgiveness] is an attempt to say: "now we understand what happened and now we are reaching a point where we can try to put it behind us." That may mean that some people

have to say "I am sorry," which is a very hard thing to do, that people have to seek amnesty for what they did and try and bring these things out in the open, not to be punished but to help break with the past. So it's okay for people to express their strong feelings and their anger but that anger mustn't be translated into revenge because then we go on and on creating bad and worse situations.[4]

For Tutu, forgiveness is not an act of laying blame but a process of reconciliation. This is accomplished by considering forgiveness as an act that has the power to create a new tomorrow, which is only possible when forgiveness is seen as a powerful instrument for reconciliation between victims and the perpetrators who wronged them. In South Africa, civil peace and the restoration of political cohesion requires a post-conflict dialogue between the wrong-doers and the victims. This is a state that insists on the human dignity of enemies, and as Mandela said, "To make peace with an enemy one must work with that enemy, and that enemy becomes one's partner."[5] There is a kind of moral transcendence to the very idea of considering an enemy as one's partner. For French-Bulgarian psychoanalyst Julia Kristeva the empathic act of forgiveness "raises the unconscious from beneath the actions and has it meet a loving other—an other who does not judge but hears my truth in the availability of love, and for that very reason allows me to be reborn."[6] Such an effort of understanding and compassion goes beyond the crime and violence that Dostoyevsky sees in the characters of Alyosha and Myshkin. Perhaps we should admit that this quality of empathy does not exist in every one of us, even though we practice other forms of reciprocity and mutuality as social beings.

Forgiveness is an act of compassion and, as Schopenhauer argues, compassion is the basis of morality.[7] There is no pride in forgiving, because forgiveness, as an inward strength, is a resistance to the lack of moral meaning in life. Seeking meaning in life is a process of overcoming the tragic sense of life. According to the Spanish philosopher Miguel de Unamuno, this tragic sense of life is the starting point of all religion and all philosophy. If Unamuno is correct in affirming that "the real and concrete truth, not the methodical and ideal, is: *homo sum, ergo cogito*. To feel oneself a man is more immediate than to think,"[8] then life does not discover that it is life until it speaks the language of compassion and forgiveness. The creative force of life receives form in what the German existentialist Karl Jaspers calls the boundary-situation of Man (*Grenzsituation*).[9] A human being is a creature that always finds itself on the boundary line between revenge and forgiveness, between hate and love. All metaphysical attitudes in life, such as those of the optimist and the pessimist, have no other foundation than this. The issue for philosophers is not whether we love or whether we hate, but why we love and why we hate. David Hume has a very illuminating point on this matter in Part III of his *Treatise on Human Nature*:

> But in the main, we may affirm, that man in general, or human nature, is nothing but the object both of love and hatred, and requires some other cause, which by a double relation of impressions and ideas, may excite these passions. In vain would we endeavour to elude this hypothesis. There are no phenomena that point out any such kind affection to men, independent of their merit, and every other circumstance. We love company in general; but it is as we love any other amusement. An Englishman in Italy is a friend: A European in China; and perhaps a man would be beloved as such, were we to meet him in the moon. But this proceeds only from the relation to ourselves; which in these cases gathers force by being confined to a few persons.[10]

From all this, it follows that our only real motive for forgiving is to vanquish suffering. The heavenly spirit of forgiveness vanquishes the devilish spirit of revenge when the rosebuds of hate and suffering turn into flames of love and forgiveness. One recalls how the ambiguous character of Faust in the prologue to Goethe's play resists Mephistopheles in order to reach for the stars beyond his sufferings: "A good man, though his striving be obscure, remains aware that there is one right way."[11] And Schopenhauer adds his comment on Goethe's verse in his magnum opus, *The World as Will and Representation*:

> The great Goethe has given us a distinct and visible description of this denial of the will, brought about by great misfortune and by the despair of all deliverance, in his immortal masterpiece *Faust*, in the story of the sufferings of Gretchen. I know of no other description in poetry. It is a perfect specimen of the second path, which leads to the denial of the will but not, like the first, through the mere knowledge of the suffering of the whole world which one acquires voluntarily, but through the excessive pain felt in one's own person. It is true that many tragedies bring their violently willing heroes ultimately to this point of complete resignation, and then the will-to-live and its phenomenon usually end at the same time. But no description known to me brings to

us the essential point of that conversion so dis-
tinctly and so free from everything extraneous
as the one mentioned in *Faust*.[12]

More accurately, Schopenhauer underlines: "Thus, that
there is no ultimate aim of striving means that there is
no measure or end of suffering."[13]

The long pathway of history is paved with the suffering
of humanity and with our striving to overcome them. In
the past, humanity had a clear manifestation of forgiveness
in the divine gesture. Today, as we saw in the example of
the post-apartheid experience in South Africa, forgiveness is no longer a purely divine matter. It is a social and
political attitude of the mind. For those who no longer
believe, the light that heals shines not from the divine
actions of God or gods, but from those of a social-historical human being. Forgiveness is history's burden and it
cannot be thrown off for fear of the demons of revenge.
However, forgiving is not necessarily giving in. It is not
a compromise with the world of mediocrity. But how can
we live in a world like ours without compromising with
it? The answer is simple: by striving for a spirit that can
give meaning to our "living together." Forgiveness is the
very condition of this "living together." Seeking forgiveness in history is putting an end to the "knot of rancour."
Forgiveness, therefore, is an urgent global question, or

perhaps an irreplaceable response to those who call for revenge. Maybe this is why, as imperfect as it remains, the concept of forgiveness stands on the horizon of all philosophical and political evolutions that might provide the global inspiration to prevail over the impossible. It is important to understand that we become prisoners of the impossible when we are condemned to forgetfulness.

George Santayana's words are worth remembering: "Progress, far from consisting in change, depends on retentiveness ... Those who cannot remember the past are condemned to repeat it."[14] Forgiveness, therefore, is a commitment to memory and truth. It is a project of reconciliation through moral repair. It is the promise of a new beginning without forgetfulness. Finally, forgiveness is the recognition of our "shared fallibility." We are all possible wrongdoers because we are all fallible creatures. Thus, everyone suffers because no one is perfect.

Much more should be said about the imperfection that individuals, nations, and humanity try to hide and cast into oblivion, and yet I hope to have shown that the act of forgiving is fundamentally a perpetual effort to respond both humbly and majestically, with nobility of spirit, to a spiritless situation and to the moral and political shortcomings of our world. Acts of forgiveness and empathy cannot fully repair the brutality and cruelty of our world, but these acts cannot be ignored by our human civilization, as long as that civilization wants to remain humanitarian. In ignoring them, we would lose, once and for all, the overarching principles of our "living together," because it is in the seemingly small acts of remembering the past and forgiving the present—which accumulate to create a lifetime—that the essence of our humanity is captured. We must gather these pieces together and use them in many new ways, so that a different vision of life— what it is and what it was in the past—can be achieved. I hope that when human civilization comes to assess its past and present achievements or failings, it can remind itself of these words of Achilles in Homer's Iliad: "may strife perish from among gods and men, and anger that sets a man on to rage, though he be very wise, and that, sweeter far than trickling honey."[15]

9

To walk safely through the maze of human life, one needs
the light of wisdom and the guidance of virtue.

THE BUDDHA[1]

IT IS DIFFICULT ENOUGH TO CONTINUE PUTTING
faith in the wisdom of humanity, but to plead for forgiveness and to endeavour to practice it, going beyond
the spirit of revenge and retribution so present in our
own imperfect time, is a herculean challenge that cannot be taken lightly. Our present world suffers from an
arrogant shallowness that seems to me not merely a form
of thoughtlessness, but a bitter mockery of the greatest
achievements of human civilization. The lack of rebel-
liousness in our contemporary life is the result of our
moral downfall and our poverty of spirit. Living without
revolt means not recognizing the crucial process of life. As
Albert Camus wrote in his essay critiquing communism,

The Fastidious Assassins: "If one believes in nothing, if nothing makes sense, if we can assert no value whatsoever, everything is permissible and nothing is important."[2] Many people accept such a situation as a normal way of life. They refuse to put themselves at risk and continue living this way until it becomes unbearable. If we stop for a minute and think outside our herd consciousness, it becomes clear that such a life desperately lacks the virtues introduced by questioning. Conforming to normality, as we are asked to do on an everyday basis, is the highest stage of spiritual shallowness. In this light, philosophical rebellion, as the deepest form of critical thinking, is the movement by which individuals can protest against their existential conditions. Such rebellion is directed against that which denies individuals their nobility of spirit. It is a reaffirmation of thoughtfulness joined with a passionate rejection of its violation. Such rebellion is nonviolent and non-lethal, but it is a radical form of protest against the insignificance of our contemporary world. Lacking the need for conformity, philosophy faces the world with a rebellious sensitivity that negates violence.

We live in an age of paradoxes. We speak of forgiving and we prepare for revenge. We discuss peace and dialogue, and yet narrow-minded sectarianism and national and religious prejudices govern our thoughts and actions. We call this the time of the global village and multiculturalism, but we give very little thought to the actual nature of cultures and traditions. Priding ourselves on being civilized, we function day to day as labourers in a world market with no true knowledge of the past civilizations in whose names we create colleges, clubs, and political parties. None of us—especially those who care about the nobility of spirit and the creative genius that is so essential for the survival of what we are as human beings with a social-historical past—can ignore the multiple crises in human affairs and the dangers of the moment. If this is so, what is lacking and how can we correct it? Throughout this book, without pretending to have a prophetic recipe or a magical formula, and by referring only to my own life experience or that of others as revealed in literature, philosophy, religion, or politics, I have suggested the noble goal of forgiveness as opposed to hatred, vengeance, and resentment. I am convinced that we must seek forgiveness, whatever form it takes: we must labour to find it, rather than working for an insignificant world based on the values of greed, power, and hatred. This is a responsibility that our human civilization should accept without fear or apprehension. I do not know if it is possible to divert the future of our world in another direction, but I know that two of the most difficult things in life are accepting the errors of the past and preparing for the truths of the future. Every one of us has a different understanding of the past, but we would all like to believe that our future holds positive changes and progress in the right direction. Yet, I have no doubt that if our contemporary world is to attain maturity and common sense by moving beyond its present violent lunacy and destructive madness, it must be attuned to the aim of forgiveness and reconciliation as the condition sine qua non of living together. Creating such a world is not possible so long as we live under the menacing clouds of hatred, resentment, and revenge. Where are the avenues that encourage living together in today's world? How can we avoid naive wishful thinking and recognize the need to put ourselves at risk? Thinking must become at once an act of revolt and a form of forgiveness. In a world where politics has become the worst form of conformism, philosophy as an act of questioning reality has become a form of revolt. Philosophy's only limits are those it imposes on itself. As perhaps the purest form of rebellion, philosophy is born of a questioning that refuses to be the slave of reality. Philosophy begins with "the resolve of the will to think purely," Hegel says in *The Encyclopaedia Logic.*[3] Thinking purely means thinking only of the process of thought itself. It is precisely in this respect that thinking always transcends the rationally constituted realm within which we find ourselves. It is by questioning the basic assumptions of our age that philosophy presents itself as thinking toward liberation. However, this liberation does not come to us in a political context, but is formulated as a form of redemption. As Theodor Adorno claims, "The only philosophy which can be responsibly practiced in the face of despair is the attempt to contemplate all things as they would present themselves from the standpoint of redemption."[4] In other words, as revenge, greed, power, and violence diminish as acceptable resolutions to the problems of human existence, the need for forgiveness as redemption becomes more urgent.

There is perhaps a philosophical redemption, of which forgiveness offers the promise, that can make our world more livable and more lovable. Philosophy, as a form of revolt, tries to give form to an act of forgiving that aspires toward a perpetual becoming. All this is to say that to reject philosophical revolt as an art of dialogue without complacency and conformity can turn all forms of living together into a violent struggle for power and can prepare the way for revenge and resentment. The result can only be a de-civilized society that cannot confront its own monsters and nightmares. It is appropriate here to return to the Camusian vision of justice: his play *Les Justes* asks us to confront a crucial problem of our time: the limits on violence when confronted with questions of morality.[5] *Les Justes* is my favourite Camus play. I first read it when I was seventeen years old and living in France. I was so impressed by Camus' powerful writing that I decided to translate it into Persian. (This translation, which was never published, is still somewhere among my belongings in Iran.) *Les Justes* is not a historical play, but all the characters are real, and the terrorist act it describes actually took place in Moscow in February 1905. Kaliayev, the real-world name of the hero of the play, is a complex character, like those we encounter in Dostoyevsky's works. In Camus' play, Kaliayev fails to kill the Grand Duke Serge, the uncle of the Tsar, after seeing several children in his carriage. In the play, a key encounter between Stepan and Kaliayev on the issues of justice and innocence reveals the ethical impasse of terrorism:

KALIAYEV: Stepan, I am ashamed of myself. However, I can't let you go on. I agreed to kill someone to destroy this dictatorship. But after what you've said, I see a new tyranny coming, which, if it was ever installed, would make me into an assassin when I am trying to be a maker of justice.

STEPAN: What would it matter if you were not a "maker of justice," if justice was done, even by assassins? You and I are nothing.

KALIAYEV: We are something and you know it well, because it's in the name of your pride that you were speaking earlier today.

STEPAN: My pride only looks at me. But the pride of men, their revolution, the injustice under which they live, that is the business of all of us.

KALIAYEV: Men do not live by justice alone.

STEPAN: When someone steals their bread, what else will they live on but justice?

KALIAYEV: On justice and innocence.

STEPAN: Innocence? Yeah, maybe I know what that is. But I chose to ignore it, and have it be ignored by millions of men, so that one day it can take on a bigger meaning.

KALIAYEV: You have to be very sure that day will come to destroy everything that makes a man willing to keep on living.

STEPAN: I am sure of it.

KALIAYEV: You can't be. To know who, me or you, is right, you'd need the sacrifice of maybe three generations and a lot of wars, terrible revolutions. When that rain of blood is dry on the earth, you and I would have been mixed with the dust for a long time.

STEPAN: Others would come then, and I salute them as my brothers.

KALIAYEV, CRYING OUT: Others ... yes! But I love those who live today, on the same earth as I do, and they're the ones I salute; I'm fighting for them and for them I'm willing to die. And for some far-off future city that I'm not sure of, I will not slap the faces of my brothers. I will not add to living injustices for a dead justice. Brothers, I want to speak frankly and at least tell you what the simplest of peasants could say: to kill children is without honour. And if someday in my life the revolution separates itself from honour, I will turn away from it. If you decide that, I will go to the exit of the theater, but I will throw myself under the horses.[6]

This scene gives dramatic form to one of the central issues in Camus' writings: is violence wrong? In answering this question, Camus distinguishes between humane revolt and murder in the name of an ideal. Unlike the words that Camus gives his Caligula, all actions are not on equal footing. For Camus, no ideal can justify murder. Unlike Mohandas Gandhi and Martin Luther King, Jr., Camus does not advocate pure nonviolence, but he attempts to demonstrate that the refusal to kill or to legitimize murder is the starting point for living together. "I, for one, am practically certain that I have made my choice. And having chosen, it seemed to me that I ought to speak, to say that I would never count myself among the people of whatever stripe who are willing to countenance murder, and I would draw whatever consequence followed from this," writes Camus in his powerful pamphlet "*Ni victimes ni bourreaux*" ("Neither Victims nor Executioners"), which calls for a move away from abstract principles in favour of the value of human dignity.[7] "Neither Victims nor Executioners" appeared serially in the autumn of 1946 in *Combat,* the daily newspaper of the Resistance, which Camus helped edit during the Nazi occupation of France and for a short time after the war. As in the case of *Les Justes*, Camus is concerned in this essay with the effects of murder, terrorism, and other forms of violence on the perpetrators, not only on their victims, recalling Kaliayev's inability to kill the children who accompany the Grand Duke. For Camus, the revolution is not a valid justification to kill and destroy his ethical beliefs. Confronted with all the evils of the world, he reveals a philosophical deadlock, since for Camus "violence is both unavoidable and unjustifiable." However, he sides with Kaliayev and not Caligula: "We are being asked to love or to hate one another or another country or people. But a few of us are only too well aware of our similarity to our fellow human beings to accept this choice."[8] It is because of the idea of a common humanity that Camus refuses to compromise his moral responsibility. He calls this position safeguarding "a dignity common to everyone." It is this dignity that, according to Camus, is crushed by the death penalty. In his capacity as an abolitionist, he writes in *Resistance, Rebellion, and Death*, "if justice has a meaning in this world … it cannot, by its very essence, divorce itself from compassion."[9] Significantly, Camus' entire thought is distinguished by such compassion, and I believe this is how he tried to bring light into the darkness of his time; and yet he is conscious—as a private individual—of the difficulty of his task:

> Like everyone I have tried, as best I could, to improve my nature by morality. This, alas, is what has cost me most dear. With energy, which is

something I possess, we sometimes manage to act morally, but never to be moral. The person of passion who longs for goodness yields to injustice at the very moment when (s)he speaks of justice. Human beings sometimes seem to me to be a walking injustice: I am thinking of myself. If I now have the impression that I was wrong, or that I lied in what I sometimes wrote, it is because I do not know how to make my injustice honestly known. I have doubtless never said that I was a just man. I have merely happened to say that we should try to be just, and also that such an ambition involved great toil and misery. But is this distinction so important? And can the man who does not even manage to make justice prevail in his own life preach its virtues to other people?[10]

The question Camus raises in this passage has been my lifelong concern. Camus' critical intellectualism is especially clear in relation to human shortcomings. The problem, however, is that most of us are quite comfortable lying about our moral weaknesses, and whatever humanism we claim seems scarcely to be earned. Yet, as Camus shows us, humanity's confrontation with itself is part of our common destiny as human beings. This process of self-confrontation, for good or for evil, remains one of the great challenges of all times. As history reveals, seeing the world lucidly and making the right moral choices does not change human destiny, any more than it changes Sisyphus's task of pushing the boulder up the slope. Despite all this, the idea of compassion, so intensely developed by artists and philosophers, reveals that violence and horror do not represent a truthful image of the human condition, for violence always lies, and only compassion insists on speaking its mind. Perhaps what Camus called the "feverish nature of the time" invites us to share our horror of the evil that manifests through all forms of revenge and retaliation.

The question, then, is how to confront the misery and horror of our world while serving what is left of its compassionate nature. Faced with the other, aren't we always confronted with the dilemma of dialogue or destruction? Forming an answer to this question begins with recognizing our common humanity and our shared values, and goes well beyond a continuous reinvention of our victimhood and a persistent tendency to blame the other. The latter, the symptom of an enduring fearfulness and a lack of moral courage to accept one's wrongdoings, serves to perpetuate and deepen the violence among us. In a way, dying together, more than living together, has brought us to the same fate.

In this book, I have sought to assess the complexities of such a fate. My general conviction all through its writing has been that there can be no human civilization without compassion. The ethos of shared responsibility finds its expression in the process of taming violence through the act of forgiveness. This is where we should look for a political exercise of moderation and empathy, and where a climate of cooperation and reconciliation can flourish. Today, in a world riddled by insignificance and violence, indifference can no longer be permitted. Indifference has cheapened human life. To fail to recognize this is to betray our consciences.

Forgiveness is a quality that cannot be manufactured by businessmen and politicians. It is the quality of a person pursuing decency and human dignity beyond all forms of arrogance and hostility. Its ongoing relevance makes forgiveness all the more compelling in current debates on violence, democracy, and culture. The words of Jawaharlal Nehru remind us that "the cultured mind, rooted in itself, should have its doors and windows open. It should have the capacity to understand the other's viewpoint fully, though it cannot always agree with it. The question of agreement or disagreement only arises when you understand a thing. Otherwise, it is blind negation which is not a cultured approach to any question."[11] We often suffer, in our liberal oligarchies, from this "blind negation." It requires critical power and a democratic reflex to renounce some of our traditions of thought and realize that some of our safeguards of the past that, despite what we think, have not given us civility or respectability.

So here is our problem: it is too easy, as is the case in North America and Europe, to continue talking about democracy and multiculturalism and to say to religious and ethnic minorities that they should find their own way. It takes help for a young Muslim confronted with the indifference and very often the patronizing attitude of the White Christian majority to find a place in such a world. The changing world has made young Muslims aware and proud of their full worth and dignity as human beings, but has led them to lose hope and faith in the good will of our liberal institutions. As Robert Kennedy once said, "Frustrated hope and loss of faith breed desperation,"[12] and desperate people turn to violence. However, the answer to this violence is not counter-violence: there is no violent way to suppress young people filled with anger who have lost their hope in democracy. This is not a problem of religion or culture: it is a problem of democratic evil. In democracies that lack democratic passion, the only passion is for destruction. Spinoza wrote that without passion, no human activity, though supported by reason, can prosper.[13] How can one rekindle the passion for democracy in citizens spoiled by wellbeing or

resentful because of exclusion? Since 1989 and the fall of
the Berlin Wall, liberal democracy has triumphed against
other systems of governance, but its political ascendency
around the world has not always been accompanied by
democratic passion. Democratic man is no longer an animal of political passion.

There seems to be no place in today's democratic
regimes for the politics of arguing about politics. Younger
generations with no memory of the Cold War are becoming even more apathetic about democracy. On the other
hand, John Dewey's conception of politics as the shadow
cast by big business over society seems increasingly accu-
rate as corporations continue to erode our liberal democracies.[14] In light of these problems and the mounting
evidence that all is not necessarily well with democracy,
we question what is left of democracy as a discourse and as
an institution? Experience shows us that it is very difficult
to pin down democracy to one meaning, since it means
different things to different people in different contexts.
There is a failure in "expanding" democracy or "export-
ing" it from one culture or society to another because
promoting democracy is ineffective in the absence of a
democratic culture; organizing elections is only the starting point of the democratic life of a nation. The real test
of democracy is not empowering a victorious majority
or giving the greatest liberty to the greatest number, but

in a new attitude and approach to the problem of power and violence. True democratic governance is not power over society, but power within it. If democracy equals self-rule and self-control of society, the empowerment of civil society and the collective ability to rule democratically are essential constituents of democratic governance. Where democracy is practiced, the rules of the political game are defined by the absence of violence and a set of institutional guarantees against the domineering logic of the state. Yet, the more we think about it, the more these characteristics alone seem unsatisfactory and incomplete. If democracy is no more than a set of institutional guarantees, how can citizens think about politics and struggle for the emergence of new perspectives of democratic life?

Before answering this question, we need to look at how the corruption of democracies is the result of a democratic evil. There is a specific problem with the legitimacy of violence at the heart of democracies. Looking at democratic violence necessitates recognition of the paradoxical status of democracy itself. Democracy is the process of taming violence, but democratic states and societies also produce violence. The more a democratic community develops instruments of violence, the less resistant it is to this democratic evil. Perhaps this is why the politics of nonviolence is a more valuable safeguard of democracy than the free market. No matter how much money we accumulate to provide the necessities of life and make it possible to live comfortably in a democratic society, we need more than material possessions to give meaning to our common life. If we ask ourselves why we live as if democracy matters and as if it is worth our effort, the response could be that life is more than simply the satisfaction of desires. There is an ethical horizon of responsibility without which democracy has no meaning. Václav Havel reminds us that "democracy is a system based on trust in the human sense of responsibility, which it ought to awaken and cultivate."[15] This sense of common responsibility is the key to our identity as democratic beings because it comes as a reaction to the intolerable in the name of shared human dignity and vulnerability. It is a moral effort that reveals to us the complexity, spontaneity, and heterogeneity of democracy. How one is to value and properly esteem democratic citizens is presently being debated against the backdrop of the horrors and intolerable acts of cruelty that have continued in the new millennium. Perhaps this is the reason we can never be fully satisfied with democracy as a philosophical value and as a political reality: to be so would be to forget the essence of democracy as a daily effort of civic responsibility and as a continuous struggle against the intolerable. That is why any democracy that becomes a consumer value system with no sense of responsibility beyond simple political ideals will end up becoming a community of mediocrity.

Democracy alone will never be enough: it cannot be established through elections and a constitution. Something more is necessary—an emphasis on democracy as a practice of moral thinking and moral judgment. In other words, we can never build or sustain democratic institutions if they do not have the goal of offering us the Socratic experience of politics as self-examination and dialogical exchange. After all, democracy is made by humans, and its fate is related to the human condition. The line dividing democratic action and political evil cuts through the moral choice of compassion and forgiveness. There is an apparently irreducible contradiction between the moral demands of social harmony and dialogical citizenship and the practical requirements of political conquest. Not surprisingly, politics is both an art of managing complexity or organizing the polis and of the conquest of power. In a speech delivered in 1948, Camus declared: "What the conqueror of the Right or Left seeks is not unity—which is above all the harmony of opposites—but totality, which is the stamping out of differences."[16] Of course, conquest is not an attribute of any particular civilization: it is the byproduct of a civilization's descent into barbarism. Barbarism is, more than anything else, a state of being where there are no moral standards, or, as José Ortega y Gasset expressed it, "barbarism is the absence of standards to which appeal can be made."[17] For a spirit with no values or standards, civilization is sought in vain, because no values exist beyond its own. The major problem that confronts our civilizations is their de-civilizing process, which fails to understand compassion and forgiveness.

10

The truly civilized man is always skeptical and tolerant, in this field as in all others.

H. L. MENCKEN[1]

CIVILIZATION HAS LED SOME TO EMPATHY AND OTHers to madness. Human history can be summed up in two words: creation and destruction. The *Oxford English Dictionary* defines civilization as "the action or process of civilizing or of being civilized; a developed or advanced state of human society."[2] Such a definition creates a great number of difficulties. How can we correctly identify a "developed or advanced state of human society"? Developed or advanced compared to what? What does it mean to be civilized? The same *Oxford English Dictionary* also defines the verb "to civilize" as a way "to make civil; to bring out of a state of barbarism; to instruct in the arts of life; to enlighten; to refine and polish."[3] Civilization is therefore a process of learning togetherness and an ability to tame violence. All societies, according to Norbert Elias, have civilizing processes or ways of trying to solve the problem of how persons can satisfy basic needs without "destroying, frustrating, demeaning or in other ways harming each other time and time again in their search for this satisfaction."[4] Elias focuses on the "civilizing process" that has taken place in European societies since the late Middle Ages, describing it in terms of an extension and intensification of the chains of human interdependency over the course of time. According to him, complex networks of interdependence compel their members to adopt stricter standards of control. Elias shows that the monopolization of violence in the process of state formation involved such restraints. For Elias, "rationalization" is a name for the civilizing process that compartmentalizes the various built-in drive controls. At the very core of the civilizing process, sometimes a contrary current manifests itself: while the state continues to monopolize the exercise of violence and promotes and protects the civilized modes of behaviour and expression in society, it simultaneously perpetrates massive and organized acts of extreme violence toward specific categories of its citizens.

The cornerstone of Elias's thinking is the twofold movement of rationalization and bureaucratization on the one hand, and regression, breakdown, and increasing barbarism on the other. Elias himself considered Nazi violence to be symptomatic of a process of de-civilization that encouraged more widespread manifestation of brutal and violent conduct.[5] However, he also raised the possibility that civilization and de-civilization can coexist simultaneously in the formation of the modern state. For example, the monopolization of physical force by the state, through the military and the police, has a Janus-faced character. One is reminded of Elias Canetti's premonitory saga of the de-civilizing process that is played out around the library of his protagonist, Peter Kien, in his novel *Auto Da Fé*. Canetti points to the rise of Fascism and to book burning as timeless metaphors, and he warns against the perils of rationalization.[6] Canetti's idea of civilizations seems to be that history is composed of two elements: the crowd and power. Canetti defines the crowd as created by an addition of small units into a large ensemble, causing it to become something entirely different from its constituent parts. "In the crowd," writes Canetti, "the individual feels he is transcending the limits of his own person. He has a sense of relief, for the distances are removed which used to throw him back on himself and shut him in."[7] How a crowd is formed is an interesting sociological phenomenon that Canetti describes in *Crowds and Power*. The power highlighted in the title of the book is not power over masses; rather, it is the power of masses.

For Canetti, it is not the leaders who exploit the masses, but the masses that exploit the leaders. By affirming this, Canetti was reacting to the "Nuremberg alibi" that the German people were only "obeying orders" under the Nazi regime. The holocaust thus becomes a paradigm of Canetti's vision of mass society as nothing but a de-civilizing process. In mass violence, criminals become undifferentiated. By dehumanizing their victims, the killers are also dehumanized. By destroying their victims, mass killers self-destroy. They participate in the de-civilizing process of humanity that makes it possible for mass crime to be committed and repeated in the name of religion, politics, or science. There is a universal dynamic of extreme violence. History shows us that civilization is not and can never be sustainable. Civilization originates from violence and civilization returns to violence. Violence begets violence. Peace is always denied to those who use violence. There is no such thing as a "good war" against "bad guys." If this is so, what does it mean that the war on terror is being imagined through an updating of the paradigm of the good war? In *The Clash of Civilizations and the Remaking of World Order*, Samuel Huntington sees the "clash of civilizations" as a self-conscious effort to respond to the configurations of power in the world arena by formulating a post-Cold War paradigm. The "war against terror" illustrates what Huntington predicted as the "West vs Islam." Huntington's central argument is that "clashes of civilizations are the greatest threat to world peace," and that "in the post-Cold War world the most important distinctions among peoples are not ideological, political and economic. They are cultural."[8] In other words, cultural and civilizational identities are responsible for shaping the patterns of conflict. These inter-civilizational conflicts have replaced the main conflicts between the communists and capitalists of the Cold War.

Huntington's thesis of "clash of civilizations" was an early warning to American policymakers that they needed to defuse the rising "hate of the West" in the Muslim world.[9] It is true that hatred of the West and resistance to westernization have a strong position in the world today, especially in the Muslim world. It would be a mistake to see the tragedy of 9/11 as the adventurous exploit of several psychotic madmen who had decided to bring the World Trade Center down. The annihilation of the Twin Towers and the people inside them was neither an act of heroism (as it was portrayed in parts of the Muslim world) nor an act of lunacy: it was an attack against the basic idea of "civilization" as it is understood in all religions and cultures. This is more than simple distaste for some aspects of modern Western or American culture, a distaste that can be found in many cultures, even in America. It would be misleading to consider the desire to declare war on the

West, which crops up in the thinking of radical Islamists, as motivated only by a dislike for Western modernity. The young men who brought the Twin Towers down were well educated and had modern training. Their act of revenge was not against global corporate capitalism or Western imperialism, but against a "sinful" and "immoral" civilization that they believed was doomed. The last will and testament of Mohammed Atta, one of the ringleaders of the attacks, stipulates that no women be allowed to mourn him, attend his funeral, or even go near his grave. He disdained his own body so greatly that he stipulated that the man who was to wash his genitals after his death wear gloves, so that his impure sexual parts would theoretically remain untouched.

Atta's requests are echoes of what an early church father, Tertullian, proclaimed in 200 CE: "Woman (is) the obstacle to purity, the temptress, the enemy ... her body is the gate of hell."[10] In both cases, the obsession with impossible purity goes hand in hand with ideas of the imperfection of human civilization. Historically, Muslims do not hate civilization; on the contrary, Islam gave rise to many of the greatest instances of human civilization. At a time when most of the continent was shrouded in the Dark Ages, the Muslim city of Cordoba was the most advanced city in Europe. In philosophy, architecture, mathematics, astronomy, medicine, poetry, theology, and numerous other fields of human endeavour, medieval Islam was the world's most advanced civilization. And yet, the Cordoba experience is not the path taken by the radical followers of Islam today. The paradigm at work in Cordoba was that of *convivencia* and mutual dialogue. The example of Cordoba is special because it was a city that belonged to everyone because it belonged to no one. Cordoba was a city of all beliefs and all cultures. It was a city committed to a spirit of intercultural dialogue, a commitment that gave shape to its specific texture. Very few cities in today's world can, like Cordoba, so deeply experience their diversity as a sense of belonging and as a form of solidarity among differences. This intercultural perspective gave Cordoba a unique historical opportunity to pluralize its identity. Cordoba was also a humanly tempered city with an intellectual commitment to history and coexistence. Walk down the streets of Cordoba today and you really do walk in the footsteps of giants like Averroes, Maimonides, and many others who contributed to the universal knowledge of mankind. The city existed in a permanent process of mutual learning. As such, Cordoba represents a paradigm of recognition and harmony for those in search of ways to share their differences with others. Its spirit was greater than the sum of its differences.

The question, therefore, is not to oppose the West to the Rest and to speak in the manner of Christian fundamentalists of a crusade against Islam, nor to declare in a Huntingtonian tone that "there is indeed a worldwide clash going on among cultures."[11] This is not to say that religious extremism is not an issue that we must face when attempting to create amity and dialogue among cultures. However, most of the barbarities in the world are sustained in the name of a reductionist view of civilization and humanity. This process of degradation and de-civilization is founded most notably on the presumption that to be human means to belong to a religious division, an unquestioning acceptance of religious or cultural classifications as the unique and fundamental modes of representing humanity and civilization that negate the important features of human commonality. This negation is what Shylock attempts to overcome in Shakespeare's *The Merchant of Venice*:

> Hath not a Jew eyes? Hath not a Jew hands, organs, dimensions, senses, affections, passions; fed with the same food, hurt with the same weapons, subject to the same diseases, heal'd by the same means, warm'd and cool'd by the same winter and summer as a Christian is? If you prick us, do we not bleed? If you tickle us, do we not laugh? If you poison us, do we not die? And if you wrong us, shall we not revenge? If we are like you in the rest, we will resemble you in that.[12]

What Shakespeare teaches us is that for human solidarity to be able to fulfill its potential, it must take root in a world whose members—or at least a large majority—share the same moral values. There is no human solidarity without mutual respect and mutual commitment. It is often the search for negotiation, where each side makes concessions to the other, that paves the way to managing social, political, and cultural tensions in our world. The art of negotiation involves coming up with a way in which we can live together. It enables people in a society or in a global world to reconcile their interests and needs and to find areas of mutual respect and recognition. Reciprocal recognition, which flourishes through the concepts of compassion and forgiveness, is the true paradigm of intersubjectivity in our world, a symbiosis among ontological harmonies that replaces any forms of hierarchical pluralism. Although we have succeeded in achieving the affirmation of differences required by the ethical dimension of interhuman relations, it is clear that reciprocal recognition between the West and the Rest is possible only if each side renounces trying to curtail the other's possibilities and acknowledges the other, allowing each to live its otherness. This is what Hegel called *bei sich im anderen zu sein*,[13] "being self in relation to the other." Many would consider this ethic of empathy and recognition to be madness in light of our contemporary concerns, but this philosophical madness may be the spark that will light our way to overcoming a much larger madness in our world, the madness of violence.

Epilogue

The world we see that seems so insane is the result of a belief system that is not working. To perceive the world differently, we must be willing to change our belief system, let the past slip away, expand our sense of now, and dissolve the fear in our minds.

ATTRIBUTED TO WILLIAM JAMES[1]

"THE QUESTION IS NOT WHAT YOU LOOK AT—BUT how you look & whether you see," wrote Henry David Thoreau in his 1851 Journal.[2] How was I supposed to look at my past experiences, especially those that had left me filled with bitterness, and see no signs of resentment or desire for revenge? When I was freed from jail ten years ago, vengeance was certainly not the first thing that came to my mind. The memories of the hardship and suffering in solitary confinement arose not as a sudden burst of wounds in my heart but as a ringing of bells announcing the funeral of violence. I remembered the moving words that Nelson Mandela is reported to have said on the day of his freedom after twenty-seven years of imprisonment: "As I walked out the door toward the gate that would lead to my freedom, I knew if I didn't leave my bitterness and hatred behind, I'd still be in prison."[3] Great men give rise to great hopes, but they can also show us the path of wisdom and nonviolence. What Mandela achieved was a miracle of compassion. He tried to eradicate the evil that exists in our minds and hearts because he knew that forgiveness and violence can never be bedfellows. Forgiving is giving up our perceived right to harm someone for harming us.

It goes without saying that if we use violence and adopt a vengeful attitude toward our enemies, our own dignity and liberty are diminished. If we do not bring about lasting communal harmony, the day may come when no one among us will be safe from an endless cycle of resentment and retaliation. We must act, therefore, not only for the sake of our own interests and to overcome our own desire for revenge, but for all humanity. We must remember that the history of humanity has always been marked by violence and that people around the world are always faced with horrendous wrongdoing. Centuries of violence, conflict, murder, and genocide have created a general human trauma that requires healing, peacemaking, and justice, but justice and peace cannot be partners without the vision of forgiveness. This is why forgiveness is more than a simple event: it is a paradigm shift to a new outlook on human affairs. Forgiveness is the process of the moral education of humanity. Such an educative process is not possible without the transformation of cultures of violence in our societies, but the attempt to overcome cultures of violence on a daily basis involves nonviolence as a counter-culture.

To remember an act of violence and to condemn it is to struggle against it, whether there are individuals who were directly or indirectly harmed by it or who directly or indirectly organized it. As memories are passed down from generation to generation, they seem to lose their power to evoke the suffering endured by a group at a certain point in history. The way a society internalizes its collective memories of political violence and overcomes it through an act of truthfulness thus becomes a salient feature in considering the possibility of non-violent action among citizens. Simply put, one needs to explore the link between the historical collective memory of violence and how this memory figures in the violent practices of collective political action. It took humanity a long time to embrace an accountability imperative instead of vengeance as the appropriate fate for perpetrators of political repression and mass murder. However, it goes without saying that this accountability imperative involves a complex blending of multiple mechanisms. Despite the creation of institutions such as the International Criminal Court and the various ad hoc international or internationalized tribunals that attempt to harmonize modalities of justice and truth production, the preference for retributive trials in many political cultures may facilitate new atrocities and endanger the democratic transition. Even more problematic is the connection between the cultural particularities of each transitional society and transitional justice mechanisms, such as truth commissions, vetting, reparations, and memorialization.

Transitional justice is more than a simple stoic coexistence or grudging cohabitation. Transitional justice is about embracing the complexity of truth, justice, and transition in post-dictatorial societies from a nonviolent perspective. The transitional justice project aims to confront centuries-old violent modes of behaviour—political repression, conflict and war, the abuse of women and children—and contribute to the prevention of future violence and crimes. A now commonplace argument is that an inability or unwillingness to adopt truth and justice policies during periods of transition results in the past continuing to haunt the present and the repetition of past mistakes. Today, the Gandhian moment of nonviolence has become an ethical standard around the world, and with a few exceptions, restorative justice and forgiveness have brought together all stakeholders. The creative education of mankind by forgiveness creates history—that is, human time—but forgiveness is also trans-historical, which is why it transcends periods and generations. That sufficient time and commitment are available to arrive at forgiveness is the wager of human existence and human history. As Archbishop Desmond Tutu affirmed in the context of the South African Truth and Reconciliation Commission, "It is ultimately in our own best interests that we become forgiving, repentant, reconciling and reconciled people, because without forgiveness, without reconciliation, we have no future."[4] While some follow Tutu, others think that what he suggests is madness. But, as the eponymous Zorba says in the film version of *Zorba the Greek*, "A man needs a little madness, or else ... he never dares cut the rope and be free."[5]

If there is only one beautiful madness in the world that can free us from all forms of political and religious lunacy, it is the act of forgiving the person while not forgetting the event. As such, forgiveness as a new beginning does not occur when the past is forgotten or hidden in a corner of our mind; it takes place when our past sufferings are not repeated and we do not repeat each other's crimes.

This is when we enter the stage of history not from the backstage door, but by being fully present in the Agora in order to predict horror and warn others about it.

ACKNOWLEDGEMENTS

THIS BOOK WOULD NOT HAVE BEEN POSSIBLE WITH-
out the advice, support, friendship, and love of many people. First and foremost, I would like to thank my friend
and publisher Bruce Walsh, who gave me the idea of writing this book during a trip to Prague in 2013. Great thanks
go to Donna Grant, Senior Editor and Managing Editor at University of Regina Press, for her help in editing
this book. I would like to acknowledge the collaborative
work with Modern Stage Company on a project about
"Forgiveness." Many thanks go to my friend, the stage
director Soheil Parsa, for providing me with the opportunity to collaborate with MSC. I am also indebted to my
Gandhian fellows and friends PV Rajagopal (Rajaji) and
Jill Carr-Harris, with whom I have shared many dialogues
and workshops on the subject; I have benefited from their
insights. Also, this work would not have been possible

without the advice of my mother, Khojasteh Kia, who read the manuscript several times and made constructive suggestions. Finally, I would like to thank my wife, Azin, for standing beside me throughout my ordeal and the writing of this book. She has been my inspiration and motivation for moving forward. She is my rock, and I dedicate this book to her.

NOTES

Epigraph

1   Martin Luther King, Jr., "Loving Your Enemies," in Strength to Love (Minneapolis: Fortress Press, 1977), 53.

Preface

1   C. R. Haines, ed. and trans., *Marcus Aurelius* (Cambridge: Harvard University Press, 1930), 133.

2   Albert Camus, *Resistance, Rebellion, and Death*, trans. Justin O'Brien (New York: Vintage Books, 1960), 197.

3   William Butler Yeats, *Responsibilities, and other poems* (New York: MacMillan, 1916), epigraph. The epigraph is attributed to an "old play."

4   Samuel Johnson, *A Dictionary of the English Language*, vol. 2 (London: 1786), 454.

5   Charlotte Brontë, *Jane Eyre* (New York: E.P. Dutton & Co Inc, 1908), 32.

6   Ramin Jahanbegloo, *Conversations with Isaiah Berlin* (New York: Scribner, 1992), 107–108.

Chapter 1

1   Thomas Szasz, *The Second Sin* (New York: Doubleday, 1973), 51.

2   See, for example, Robert Green Ingersoll, *The Works of Robert G. Ingersoll*, vol. 2, ed. Herman E. Kittredge (New York: The Dresden Publishing Group, 1909), 322.

3   G. K. Chesterton, "Christmas and Salesmanship," in *The Collected Works of G.K. Chesterton, Vol 37: The Illustrated London News, 1935–1936* (San Francisco: Ignatius Press, 2012), 206–208.

4   William Shakespeare, *As You Like It*, 2.7.138–140.

5   Michel Foucault, *Discipline and Punish*, trans. Alan Sheridan (New York: Vintage, 1995), 293.

6   Adolf Hitler, *Mein Kampf*, trans. Ralph Manheim (Boston: Houghton Mifflin Harcourt, 1941), 313.

7   Hannah Arendt, *The Origins of Totalitarianism* (New York: Harcourt, 1973), 439.

8   Henry David Thoreau, "Civil Disobedience," in *Walden, Civil Disobedience, and Other Writings*, ed. Owen Thomas, (New York: W.W. Norton, 2008), 231.

9   Thomas Brickhouse and Nicholas Smith, *Plato's Socrates* (Oxford: Oxford University Press, 2002), 235.

10   Martin Luther King, Jr., *Why We Can't Wait* (Boston: Beacon Press, 2011), 59.

11   Victor Emil Frankl, *The Doctor and the Soul: From Psychotherapy to Logotherapy*, trans. Richard and Clara Winston (New York: Random House, 1986), 26.

12   Mohandas K. Gandhi, "Meaning of Non-Violence," *Harijan* (Poona), vol. 3, no. 23 (July 20, 1935): 180.

13   Francis Bacon, *Essays, Civil and Moral: and The New Atlantis* (New York: P.F. Collier, 1909) 615.

14   Louis de Jaucourt, "Crainte," in *Encyclopédie, ou dictionnaire raisonné des sciences, des arts et des métiers*, eds. Denis Diderot and Jean le Rond d'Alembert, vol. 4 (Paris: André le Breton, Michel-Antoine David, Laurent Durand, and Antoine-Claude Briasson, 1751), 428–429.

15   Martin Luther King, Jr., *The Papers of Martin Luther King, Jr., Volume IV: Symbol of the Movement, January 1957–December*, eds. Clayborne Carson, Susan Carson, Adrienne Clay, Virginia Shadron, and Kieran Taylor (Berkeley: University of California Press, 2000), 266.

16 Roger Bruns, *Martin Luther King, Jr.: A Biography* (Westport: Greenwood Publishing Group, 2006), 143.

17 Martin Luther King, Jr., "Acceptance Speech," in *Les Prix Nobel en 1964*, ed. Göran Liljestrand (Stockholm: Nobel Foundation, 1965).

18 Martin Luther King, Jr., "A Christmas Sermon on Peace," in *The Lost Massey Lectures: Recovered Classics from Five Great Thinkers* (Toronto: House of Anansi, 2007), 213.

19 Martin Luther King, Jr., *The Papers of Martin Luther King, Jr., Volume III: Birth of a New Age December 1955–December 1956*, eds. Clayborne Carson, Stewart Burns, Susan Carson, Peter Holloran, and Dana L. H. Powell (Berkeley: University of California Press, 1997), 458.

20 Martin Luther King, Jr., "An Experiment in Love (1958)," in *A Testament of Hope*, ed. James M. Washington (New York: Harper Collins, 1991), 20.

21 Martin Luther King, Jr., "The Ethical Demands for Integration (1963)," in *Testament of Hope*, 122.

22 Martin Luther King, Jr., *Where Do We Go from Here?* (Boston: Beacon Press, 2010), 180–181.

23 Martin Luther King, Jr., "Where do we go from here: chaos or community (1967)," in *Testament of Hope*, 626.

24 Martin Luther King, Jr., *The Trumpet of Conscience* (New York: Harper & Row, 1967), 74–75.

Chapter 2

1 Reza Ordoubadian, trans., *The Poems of Hafez* (Bethesda, Maryland: Ibex Publishers, 2006), 182.

2 Emmanuel Levinas, *Ethics and Infinity*, trans. Richard A. Cohen (Pittsburgh: Duquesne University Press, 1985), 87.

3 Ibid, 87.

4 Aristotle, "Rhetoric" Book 2, Chapter 4, in *The Basic Works of*

Aristotle, ed. Richard McKeon (New York: Random House, 1941), 1386.

5   Gustave Le Bon, *The Psychology of Crowds* (New York: Start Publishing LLC, 2012), 61.

6   Søren Kierkegaard, *Upbuilding Discourses in Various Spirits*, eds. and trans. Howard V. Hong and Edna H. Hong (Princeton: Princeton University Press, 1993), 368.

7   Joachim Garff, *Søren Kierkegaard: A Biography* (Princeton: Princeton University Press, 2007), 484.

8   Søren Kierkegaard, "Either/or, Part 2," in *The Essential Kierkegaard*, eds. Howard V. Hong and Edna H. Hong (Princeton: Princeton University Press, 2013), 76.

9   Albert Camus, "Reflections on the Guillotine," in *Resistance Rebellion and Death* (New York: Modern Library, 1963), 22.

10 George Bernard Shaw, Preface on the Prospects of Christianity, *Androcles and the Lion* (London: Penguin Books, 1957), 19.

11 *Fury*, directed by Fritz Lang (1936; Burbank, CA: Warner Home Video, 2005), DVD.

12 William Shakespeare, *Macbeth*, 5.1.30.

Chapter 3

1   Mohandas K. Gandhi, *Non-Violence in Peace and War, Vol I* (Ahmedabad, Navajivan Publishing House, 1948), 240.

2   Pierre Manent, *A World Beyond Politics? A Defense of the Nation State* (Princeton: Princeton University Press, 2006), 115.

3   Georg Wilhelm Friedrich Hegel, *Phenomenology of Spirit*, trans. A. V. Miller (Oxford: Oxford University Press, 1977), 400.

4   Ibid, 279.

5   Judith Butler, *Antigone's Claim: Kinship Between Life and Death* (New York: Columbia University Press, 2000), 33.

6   Sophocles, *The Three Theban Plays: Antigone, Opedipus the King,*

Oedipus at Colonus, trans. Robert Fagles (London: Penguin Classics, 1984), paragraph 14441–4.

7   Hegel, *Phenomenology of Spirit*, 284.

8   George Eliot, *Middlemarch*, ed. W. J. Harvey (London: Penguin Books, 1965), 789.

9   Paul Ricoeur, *The Symbolism of Evil* (New York: Harper and Row, 1967), 102.

10 Ibid., 102.

11 Karl Jaspers, *The Question of German Guilt*, trans. E. B. Ashton (New York: Capricorn Books, 1961) 63–64.

12 Ibid., 79.

13 Ricoeur, *Symbolism of Evil*, 102.

14 Ibid., 150.

15 Martin Buber, *Martin Buber on Psychology and Psychotherapy: Essays, Letters, and Dialogue*, ed. Judith Buber Agassi (Syracuse: Syracuse University Press,1999), 116.

16 Martin Buber, *The Knowledge of Man* (New York: Harper and Row, 1965), 127.

17 John Rawls, *A Theory of Justice* (Cambridge, MA: Harvard University Press, 1971), 484.

18 Hannah Arendt, "Organized Guilt and Universal Responsibility," in *Essays in Understanding*, ed. J. Kohn (New York: Harcourt, Brace & Co., 1994), 131.

Chapter 4

1   Joseph Pearce, "An Interview with Alexander Solzhenitsyn," *St. Austin Review* 2 no. 2 (February, 2003).

2   William Shakespeare, *Macbeth*, 4.3.215–216.

3   William Shakespeare, *Hamlet*, 5.2.64–71.

4   William Shakespeare, *Julius Caesar*, 5.3.193–95.

5   William Shakespeare, *Othello*, 5.2.96–97.

6   Ibid., 5.2.99.

7   Ibid., 5.2.300.

8   Phyllis Chesler, "Worldwide Trends in Honor Killing," *Middle East Quarterly* 17, no. 2 (Spring 2010): 3.

9   William W. E. Slights, "The Sacrificial Crisis in *Titus Andronicus*," *University of Toronto Quarterly* 49, no. 1 (1979): 18–32.

10   William Shakespeare, *Titus Andronicus*, 5.3.72.

11   William Blake, *The Complete Poetry and Prose of William Blake* (Berkley: University of California Press, 1982), 589.

12   Abdul Ghaffar Khan, 1985 interview, in *An Unknown Legend of India: A bharat ratna,* Guarev Pundeer (Munich: BookRix, 2015), 27.

Chapter 5

1   Martin Luther King, Jr., "Martin Luther King and Economic Justice, 1966," in *Hearings Before the Subcommittee on Executive Reorganization of the Committee on Government Operations, United States Senate, Eighty-Ninth Congress, Second Session, December 14 and 15, 1966, Part 14* (Washington, D.C.: United States Government Printing Office, 1967), 2967–2982.

2   Tzvetan Todorov, *Facing the Extreme: Moral Life in the Concentration Camps*, trans. Arthur Denner and Abigail Pollak (New York: Metropolitan Books, 1996), 291.

3   Ibid.

4   Alexander Solzhenitsyn, *One Word of Truth* (London: Bodley Head, 1972), 127.

5   Friedrich Nietzsche, *Basic Writings of Nietzsche*, trans. Walter Kaufmann (New York: Random House, 2009), 11.

6   Sir William Lower Knight, *Horatius: A Roman Tragedie* (London, G. Bedell and T. Collins, 1656), 46–7.

7   Friedrich Nietzsche, *On the Genealogy of Morals*, ed. Keith Ansell-Pearson, trans. Carol Diethe (New York: Cambridge University Press, 2007), 21.

8   Ibid., 22.

9   Ibid., 21.

10   Ibid., 17.

11   Ibid.

12   George Orwell, "Notes on Nationalism," in *England Your England and Other Essays* (London: Secker & Warburg, 1953), 51.

13   Arendt, *Origins of Totalitarianism*, 6.

14   Ibid., 465.

15   Ibid., 471.

16   Ibid., 465.

17   Cornelius Castoriadis, *The Imaginary Institution of Society* (Cambridge, MA: Polity Press, 1987), 128.

18   Artur London, *The Confession*, trans. Alastair Hamilton (New York: William Morrow & Co., 1970).

19   Artur London, *On Trial*, trans. Alastair Hamilton (London: Macdonald & Co., 1970), 343.

20   C. Virgil Gheorghiu, *The Twenty-Fifth Hour*, trans. Rita Eldon (London: William Heinemann Ltd, 1950), ix.

21   Ibid., 373.

22   Alexandre Dumas, *The Count of Monte Cristo*, trans. David Coward (Oxford: Oxford University Press, 2008), xiii.

23   F. W. J. Hemmings, *Alexandre Dumas: The King of Romance* (London: A&C Black, 2011), chap. 2.

24   Dumas, *Count of Monte Cristo*, 490.

25   Mott T. Greene, "Writing Scientific Biography," *Journal of the History of Biology* 40, 4 (2007): 730.

26   Antonio Gramsci, *The Prison Notebooks* (London: International Publisher, 1971), 349–350.

27   Dumas, *Count of Monte Cristo*, 1082.

28   Jean-Paul Sartre, "Herman Melville's *Moby Dick*," in *Twenti-eth-Century Interpretations of Moby Dick*, ed. Michael Gilbert (Englewood Cliffs, NJ: Prentice-Hall, 1977), 94.

29   Herman Melville, *Moby-Dick; or, The Whale* (Berkley: University of California Press, 1979), 574.

30   Melville, *Moby-Dick,* 272.

31   Ibid.

32   Bruce Duffy, *Disaster Was My God: A Novel of the Outlaw Life of Arthur Rimbaud* (New York: Anchor Books, 2012), 147.

33   Melville, *Moby-Dick*, 565.

34   Lewis Mumford, *Herman Melville* (New York: Literary Guild of America, 1929), 184.

35   Melville, *Moby-Dick*, 574–575.

36   Max Scheler, *On Feeling, Knowing, and Valuing: Selected Writings*, ed. Harold Bershady (Chicago: University of Chicago Press, 1992), 192.

37   Ibid., 119.

38   Ibid.

Chapter 6

1   Thomas Merton cited in Matthew Fox, "A Spirituality Called Compassion," *Religious Education* 73, 3, (1978): 292.

2   Federico García Lorca, *Blood Wedding*, trans. Lillain Groag (New York: Dramatis Play Services, Inc., 2002), 28.

3   John Brande Trend, *Lorca and the Spanish Poetic Tradition* (Oxford: Russell & Russell, 1956), 15.

4   Alfred Lord Tennyson, "Ulysses" in *The Complete Works of Alfred Tennyson* (New York: R. Worthington, 1879), 62.

5   Hannah Arendt, *On Revolution* (New York: Faber and Faber, 1963), 173.

6   Hannah Arendt, *The Human Condition* (Chicago: University of Chicago Press, 1958), 237.

7   Arendt, *Human Condition,* 237.

8   Luke. 23:34.

9   Mark 2:10.

10 Arendt, *Human Condition*, 239.

11 Mark 14:24.

12 Matt. 26:28.

13 Mark 2:10.

14 Mark 3:28.

15 Luke 7:47.

16 Matt. 6:14–15.

17 Peter Khoroche, trans., *Once the Buddha Was a Monkey: Ārya Śūra's Jātakamālā* (Chicago: University of Chicago Press, 1989), 185.

18 Homer, *Iliad, Volume II: Books 13–24*, trans. A. T. Murray (Cambridge, MA: Harvard University Press, 1999), 471–473.

19 Maimonides, *Guide of the Perplexed, Volume 3*, trans. Shlomo Pines (Chicago: University of Chicago Press, 1963), 10.

20 Vladimir Jankélévitch, "Should We Pardon Them?," trans. Ann Hobart, *Critical Inquiry* 22, 3 (1996): 567.

21   Vladimir Jankélévitch, *Forgiveness*, trans. Andrew Kelley (Chicago: University of Chicago Press, 2005), 162.

22   Jankélévitch, "Should We Pardon Them?," 567.

23   Alan Udoff, ed., *Vladimir Jankélévitch and the Question of Forgiveness* (Lanham: Lexington Books, 2013), 152.

24   Udoff, *Vladimir Jankélévitch*, 208.

25   Jacques Derrida, *On Cosmopolitanism and Forgiveness*, trans. Mark Dooley and Michael Hughes (New York: Routledge, 2001), 51.

Chapter 7

1   His Holiness the Dalai Lama and Howard C. Cutler, M. D., *The Art of Happiness: A Handbook for Living* (New York: Riverhead Books, 1998), 119.

2   Max Stirner, *The Ego and Its Own* (New York: Boni and Liveright, Inc., 1918), 134.

3   Friedrich Nietzsche, *On the Genealogy of Morals and Ecce Homo*, trans. Walter Kaufmann (New York: Vintage, 2010), 287.

4   Nikolai Berdyaev, *The Divine and the Human*, trans. R. M. French (London: Geoffrey Bles, 1949), 65.

5   Pierre Bourdieu, *Pascalian Meditations* (Stanford: Stanford University Press, 2000), 33.

6   Fyodor Dostoyevsky, *The Brothers Karamazov*, trans. Constance Garnett (New York: Dover, 2005), 333.

7   Ibid., 222.

8   Ibid., 261.

9   Paul Ricoeur, "Forward," in Stephen Strasser, *Phenomenology of Feeling* (Pittsburgh: Duquesne University Press, 1977), xiv.

10   *La legge è legge (The Law is the Law)*, directed by Christian-Jaque (1958; Rome: Warner Home Video, 2007), DVD.

Chapter 8

1 Anthony Sampson, *Mandela: The Authorized Biography* (New York: Harper Collins, 1999), 523.

2 Immanuel Kant, *An Answer to the Question: 'What is Enlightenment?'* (New York: Penguin, 2009), 1.

3 Ps. 127:1.

4 François du Bois and Antje du Bois-Pedain, eds., *Justice and Reconciliation in Post-Apartheid South Africa* (Cambridge: Cambridge University Press, 2009), 213–214.

5 Nelson Mandela, *Long Walk to Freedom* (New York: Little Brown and Company, 1994), 112.

6 Julia Kristeva, *Black Sun: Depression and Melancholia*, trans. Leon S. Roudiez (New York: Columbia University Press, 1989), 205.

7 Arthur Schopenhauer, *On the Basis of Morality*, trans. E. F. J. Payne (Indianapolis: Bobbs-Merrill, 1965).

8 Anthony Kerrigan, *Tragic Sense of Life*, trans. Miguel de Unamuno (Princeton: Princeton University Press, 1972), 312.

9 Karl Jaspers, *Philosophie: II. Existenzerhellung* (Berlin: Springer, 2013), 210.

10 David Hume, *A Treatise of Human Nature, vol. 2* (New York: E.P. Dutton & Co Inc, 1962), 188.

11 Johann Wolfgang von Goethe, *Faust: A Tragedy Part 1*, trans. Mike Smith (Bristol, UK: Shearsman Books Ltd, 2012), 26.

12 Arthur Schopenhauer, *The World as Will and Representation*, trans. E. F. J. Payne, vol. 1 (New York: Dover Publications, Inc., 1969), 393.

13 Ibid., 309.

14 George Santayana, *Reason in Common Sense* (New York: Scribner, 1929), 172.

15   Homer, *Iliad*, 295.

Chapter 9

1   Bukkyō Dendō Kyōkai, *The Teachings of Buddha* (Moraga, CA: Sterling Publishers Pvt. Ltd, 2005), 80.

2   Albert Camus, *The Fastidious Assassins*, trans. Anthony Bower (New York: Penguin, 2008), 4.

3   Georg Wilhelm Friedrich Hegel, *The Encyclopaedia Logic*, trans. T. F. Geraets, W. A. Suchting, and H. S. Harris (Indianapolis: Hackett, 1991), 124.

4   Theodor Adorno, *Minima Moralia: Reflections on a Damaged Life*, trans. E. F. N. Jephcott (London: Verso, 1978), 247.

5   Albert Camus, *Les Justes: pièce en cinq actes* (Paris: Gallimard, 1950).

6   Ibid., 74–78.

7   Albert Camus, "November 30, 1946, Neither Victims nor Executioners, Toward Dialogue," in *Camus at Combat: Writing 1944–1947*, Jacqueline Lévi-Valensi, ed. (Princeton: Princeton University Press, 2006), 274.

8   Ibid.

9   Camus, *Resistance, Rebellion, and Death*, 217.

10   Albert Camus, *Lyrical and Critical Essays*, ed. Philip Thody, trans. Ellen Conroy Kennedy (London: Hamish Hamilton Ltd., 1967), 12.

11   Jawaharlal Nehru, *Excerpts from His Writings and Speeches* (Delhi: Ministry of Information and Broadcasting, Government of India, 1964), 80.

12   "Words of the Week," *Jet* 34, no. 11 (20 June 1968): 30.

13   Ramin Jahanbegloo, *Introduction to Nonviolence* (Basingstoke: Palgrave Macmillan, 2014), 177.

14   Noam Chomsky, "Democracy and education," *Metro Magazine: Media & Education Magazine* 102 (1995): 20–29.

15   Václav Havel, *Toward a Civil Society: Selected Speeches and Writings, 1990–1994*, ed. and trans. Paul Wilson Havel (Prague: Lidové Noviny, 1995), 261.

16   Albert Camus, "The Artist as Witness of Freedom: The Independent Mind in an Age of Ideologies [Dec. 1, 1949]," *Commentary Magazine* 8. (June 2015): para. 14.

17   José Ortega y Gasset, *The Revolt of the Masses*, (New York: New American Library, 1960), 72.

Chapter 10

1   H. L. Mencken, *Minority Report: H.L. Mencken's Notebooks* (New York: Alfred A. Knopf, 1956), 416.

2   Angus Stevenson, ed., *The Oxford Dictionary of English* (Oxford: Oxford University Press, 2010), 310.

3   Ibid.

4   Norbert Elias, *What is Sociology?* (Hutchinson: University of Michigan, 1970), 31.

5   Norbert Elias, *The Germans: Power Struggles and the Development of Habitus in the Nineteenth and Twentieth Centuries* (Cambridge: Polity Press, 1997).

6   Elias Canetti, *Auto Da Fé*, trans. C. V. Wedgwood (London: Penguin, 1965).

7   Elias Canetti, *Crowds and Power* (New York: Viking Press, 1966), 20.

8   Samuel Huntington, *The Clash of Civilizations and the Remaking of World Order* (New York: Penguin, 1997), 21.

9   Ramin Jahanbegloo, *The Clash of Intolerances* (Dehli: Har-Anand Publications, 2007), 124.

10   Wolfgang Lederer, *The Fear of Women* (New York: Grune & Stratton, 1968), 162.

11   Huntington, *Clash of Civilizations*, 213.

12   William Shakespeare, *The Merchant of Venice*, 3.1.49–57.

13   Robert R. Williams, *Hegel's Ethics of Recognition* (Berkeley: University of California Press, 1997), 84.

Epilogue

1   Eric Kalenze, *Education is Upside-Down: Reframing Reform to Focus on the Right Problems* (New York: Rowman & Littlefield, 2014), 1.

2   Henry David Thoreau, *A Year in Thoreau's Journal: 1851* (New York: Penguin Books, 1993), 146.

3   Hillary Rodham Clinton, *Living History* (Toronto: Simon & Schuster, 2003), 236.

4   Desmond Tutu, *No Future without Forgiveness* (New York, Doubleday, 1999), 244.

5   *Zorba the Greek*, directed by Michael Cacoyannis (1964; Burbank, CA: 20th Century Fox, 2004), DVD.

WORKS CITED

Adorno, Theodor. *Minima Morlia: Reflections from Damaged Life*. Translated by E. F. N. Jephcott. London: Verso, 1978.

Arendt, Hannah. *The Human Condition*. Chicago: University of Chicago Press, 1958.

———. *On Revolution*. New York: Faber and Faber, 1963.

———. "Organized Guilt and Universal Responsibility." In *Essays in Understanding*. Edited by J. Kohn. New York: Harcourt, Brace & Co., 1994.

———. *The Origins of Totalitarianism*. New York: Harcourt, 1973.

Aristotle. *The Basic Works of Aristotle*. Edited by Richard McKeon. New York: Random House, 1941.

Bacon, Francis. *Essays, Civil and Moral: and The New Atlantis*. New York: P.F. Collier, 1909.

Berdyaev, Nikolai. *The Divine and the Human*. Translated by R. M. French. London: Geoffrey Bles, 1949.

Blake, William. *The Complete Poetry and Prose of William Blake*. Berkley: University of California Press, 1982.

Bourdieu, Pierre. *Pascalian Meditations*. Stanford: Stanford University Press, 2000.

Brickhouse, Thomas, and Nicholas Smith. *Plato's Socrates*. Oxford: Oxford University Press, 2002.

Brontë, Charlotte. *Jane Eyre*. New York: E.P. Dutton & Co Inc, 1908.

Bruns, Roger. *Martin Luther King, Jr.: A Biography*. Westport: Greenwood Publishing Group, 2006.

Buber, Martin. *The Knowledge of Man*. New York: Harper and Row, 1965.

———. *Martin Buber on Psychology and Psychotherapy: Essays, Letters, and Dialogue*. Edited by Judith Buber Agassi. Syracuse: Syracuse University Press, 1999.

Butler, Judith. *Antigone's Claim: Kinship Between Life and Death*. New York: Columbia University Press, 2000.

Camus, Albert. *The Fastidious Assassins*. Translated by Anthony Bower. New York: Penguin, 2008.

———. *Les Justes: pièce en cinq actes*. Paris: Gallimard, 1950.

———. *Lyrical and Critical Essays*. Edited by Philip Thody. Translated by Ellen Conroy Kennedy. London: Hamish Hamilton Ltd., 1967.

———. "November 30, 1946, Neither Victims nor Executioners, Toward Dialogue." In *Camus at Combat: Writing 1944–1947*. Edited by Jacqueline Lévi-Valensi. Princeton: Princeton University Press, 2006.

———. "Reflections on the Guillotine." In *Resistance Rebellion and Death*. New York: Modern Library, 1963.

———. "The Artist as Witness of Freedom: The Independent Mind in an Age of Ideologies [Dec. 1, 1949]." *Commentary Magazine* 8. (June 2015).

———. *Resistance, Rebellion, and Death*. Translated by Justin O'Brien. New York: Vintage Books, 1960.

Canetti, Elias. *Auto Da Fé*. Translated by C. V. Wedgwood. London: Penguin Books, 1965.

———. *Crowds and Power*. New York: Viking Press, 1966.

Castoriadis, Cornelius. *The Imaginary Institution of Society*. Cambridge, MA: Polity Press, 1987.

Chesler, Phyllis. "Worldwide Trends in Honor Killing." *Middle East Quarterly* 17, no. 2 (Spring 2010): 3–11.

Chesterton, G. K. "Christmas and Salesmanship." In *The Collected Works of G.K. Chesterton, Vol 37: The Illustrated London News, 1935–1936*. San Francisco: Ignatius Press, 2012.

Chomsky, Noam. "Democracy and education," *Metro Magazine: Media & Education Magazine* 102 (1995): 20–29.

Clinton, Hillary Rodham. *Living History.* Toronto: Simon & Schuster, 2003.

Derrida, Jacques. *On Cosmopolitanism and Forgiveness.* Translated by Mark Dooley and Michael Hughes. New York: Routledge, 2001.

Dostoyevsky, Fyodor. *The Brothers Karamazov.* Translated by Constance Garnett. New York: Dover, 2005.

du Bois, François, and Antje du Bois-Pedain, eds. *Justice and Reconciliation in Post-Apartheid South Africa.* Cambridge: Cambridge University Press, 2009.

Duffy, Bruce. *Disaster Was My God: A Novel of the Outlaw Life of Arthur Rimbaud.* New York: Anchor Books, 2012.

Dumas, Alexandre. *The Count of Monte Cristo.* Translated by David Coward. Oxford: Oxford University Press, 2008.

Elias, Norbert. *The Germans: Power Struggles and the Development of Habitus in the Nineteenth and Twentieth Centuries.* Cambridge: Polity Press, 1997.

———. *What is Sociology?* Hutchinson: University of Michigan, 1970.

Eliot, George. *Middlemarch.* Edited by W. J. Harvey. London: Penguin Books, 1965.

Foucault, Michel. *Discipline and Punish.* Translated by Alan Sheridan. New York: Vintage, 1995).

Frankl, Victor Emil. *The Doctor and the Soul: From Psychotherapy to Logotherapy.* Translated by Richard and Clara Winston. New York: Random House, 1986.

Fury. Directed by Fritz Lang. 1936. Burbank, CA: Warner Home Video, 2005.

Gandhi, Mohandas K. "Meaning of Non-Violence." *Harijan* (Poona), vol. 3, no. 23 (July 20, 1935): 180–181.

————. *Non-Violence in Peace and War, Vol I*. Ahmedabad, Navajivan Publishing House, 1948.

Garff, Joachim. *Søren Kierkegaard: A Biography*. Princeton: Princeton University Press, 2007.

Gasset, José Ortega y. *The Revolt of the Masses*. New York: New American Library, 1960.

Gheorghiu, C. Virgil. *The Twenty-Fifth Hour*. Translated by Rita Eldon. London: William Heinemann Ltd, 1950.

Goethe, Johann Wolfgang von. *Faust: A Tragedy Part 1*. Translated by Mike Smith. Bristol, UK: Shearsman Books Ltd, 2012.

Gramsci, Antonio. *The Prison Notebooks*. London: International Publisher, 1971.

Greene, Mott T. "Writing Scientific Biography." *Journal of the History of Biology* 40, 4 (2007): 727–759.

Haines, C. R., ed. and trans. *Marcus Aurelius*. Cambridge: Harvard University Press, 1930.

Havel, Václav. *Toward a Civil Society: Selected Speeches and Writings, 1990–1994*. Edited and translated by Paul Wilson Havel. Prague: Lidové Noviny, 1995.

Hegel, Georg Wilhelm Friedrich. *The Encyclopaedia Logic*. Translated by T. F. Geraets, W. A. Suchting, and H. S. Harris. Indianapolis: Hackett, 1991.

————. *Phenomenology of Spirit*. Translated by A. V. Miller. Oxford: Oxford University Press, 1977.

Hemmings, F. W. J. *Alexandre Dumas: The King of Romance*. London: A&C Black, 2011.

His Holiness the Dalai Lama and Howard C. Cutler, M. D. *The Art of Happiness: A Handbook for Living*. New York: Riverhead Books, 1998.

Hitler, Adolf. *Mein Kampf*. Translated by Ralph Manheim. Boston: Houghton Mifflin Harcourt, 1941.

Homer. *Iliad, Volume II: Books 13–24.* Translated by A. T. Murray. Cambridge, MA: Harvard University Press, 1999.

Hume, David. *A Treatise of Human Nature, Vol. 2.* New York: E.P. Dutton & Co Inc, 1962.

Huntington, Samuel. *The Clash of Civilizations and the Remaking of World Order.* New York: Penguin, 1997.

Ingersoll, Robert Green. *The Works of Robert G. Ingersoll*, vol. 2. Edited by Herman E. Kittredge. New York: The Dresden Publishing Group, 1909.

Jahanbegloo, Ramin. *The Clash of Intolerances.* Dehli: Har-Anand Publications, 2007.

———. *Conversations with Isaiah Berlin.* New York: Scribner, 1992.

———. *Introduction to Nonviolence.* Basingstoke: Palgrave Macmillan, 2014.

Jankélévitch, Vladimir. *Forgiveness.* Translated by Andrew Kelley. Chicago: University of Chicago Press, 2005.

———. "Should We Pardon Them?" Translated by Ann Hobart. *Critical Inquiry* 22, 3 (1996): 552–572.

Jaspers, Karl. *The Question of German Guilt.* Translated by E. B. Ashton. New York: Capricorn Books, 1961.

———. *Philosophie: II. Existenzerhellung.* Berlin: Springer, 2013.

de Jaucourt, Louis. "Crainte." In *Encyclopédie, ou dictionnaire raisonné des sciences, des arts et des métiers*, edited by Denis Diderot and Jean le Rond d'Alembert, vol. 4: 428–429. Paris: André le Breton, Michel-Antoine David, Laurent Durand, and Antoine-Claude Briasson, 1751.

Johnson, Samuel. *A Dictionary of the English Language*, vol. 2. London: 1786.

Kalenze, Eric. *Education is Upside-Down: Reframing Reform to Focus on the Right Problems.* New York: Rowman & Littlefield, 2014.

Kant, Immanuel. *An Answer to the Question: 'What is Enlightenment?'* New York: Penguin, 2009.

Kerrigan, Anthony. *Tragic Sense of Life.* Translated by Miguel de Unamuno. Princeton: Princeton University Press, 1972.

Khan, Abdul Ghaffar. 1985 interview. In *An Unknown Legend of India: A bharat ratna,* Guarev Pundeer. Munich: BookRix, 2015.

Khoroche, Peter, trans. *Once the Buddha Was a Monkey:* Ārya Śūra's Jātakamālā. Chicago: University of Chicago Press, 1989.

Kierkegaard, Søren. "Either/or, Part 2." In *The Essential Kierkegaard,* edited by Howard V. Hong and Edna H. Hong. Princeton: Princeton University Press, 2013.

———. *Upbuilding Discourses in Various Spirits.* Edited and translated by Howard V. Hong and Edna H. Hong. Princeton: Princeton University Press, 1993.

King, Jr., Martin Luther. "Acceptance Speech." In *Les Prix Nobel en 1964,* edited by Göran Liljestrand. Stockholm: Nobel Foundation, 1965.

———. "A Christmas Sermon on Peace." In *The Lost Massey Lectures: Recovered Classics from Five Great Thinkers,* 209–217. Toronto: House of Anansi, 2007.

———. "The Ethical Demands for Integration (1963)." In *A Testament of Hope,* edited by James M. Washington. New York: Harper Collins, 1991.

———. "An Experiment in Love (1958)." In *A Testament of Hope,* edited by James M. Washington. New York: Harper Collins, 1991.

———. "Loving Your Enemies." In *Strength to Love.* Minneapolis: Fortress Press, 1977.

———. "Martin Luther King and Economic Justice, 1966." In *Hearings Before the Subcommittee on Executive Reorganization of the Committee on Government Operations, United States Senate, Eighty-Ninth Congress, Second Session, December 14 and 15, 1966, Part 14,* 2967–2982. Washington, D.C.: United States Government Printing Office, 1967.

————. *The Papers of Martin Luther King, Jr., Volume III: Birth of a New Age December 1955–December 1956*. Edited by Clayborne Carson, Stewart Burns, Susan Carson, Peter Holloran, and Dana L. H. Powell. Berkeley: University of California Press, 1997.

————. *The Papers of Martin Luther King, Jr., Volume IV: Symbol of the Movement, January 1957–December*. Edited by Clayborne Carson, Susan Carson, Adrienne Clay, Virginia Shadron, and Kieran Taylor. Berkeley: University of California Press, 2000.

————. *The Trumpet of Conscience*. New York: Harper & Row, 1967.

————. "Where do we go from here: chaos or community (1967)." In *A Testament of Hope*, edited by James M. Washington. New York: Harper Collins, 1991.

————. *Where Do We Go from Here?* Boston: Beacon Press, 2010.

————. *Why We Can't Wait*. Boston: Beacon Press, 2011.

Knight, Sir William Lower. *Horatius: A Roman Tragedie*. London, G. Bedell and T. Collins, 1656.

Kristeva, Julia. *Black Sun: Depression and Melancholia*. Translated by Leon S. Roudiez. New York: Columbia University Press, 1989.

Kyōkai, Bukkyō Dendō. *The Teachings of Buddha*. Moraga, CA: Sterling Publishers Pvt. Ltd, 2005.

La legge è legge (The Law is the Law). Directed by Christian-Jaque. 1958. Rome: Warner Home Video, 2007.

Le Bon, Gustave. *The Psychology of Crowds*. New York: Start Publishing LLC, 2012.

Lederer, Wolfgang. *The Fear of Women*. New York: Grune & Stratton, 1968.

Levinas, Emmanuel. *Ethics and Infinity*. Translated by Richard A. Cohen. Pittsburgh: Duquesne University Press, 1985.

London, Artur. *The Confession*. Translated by Alastair Hamilton. New York: William Morrow & Co., 1970.

———. *On Trial.* Translated by Alastair Hamilton. London: Macdonald & Co., 1970.

Lorca, Federico García. *Blood Wedding.* Translated by Lillain Groag. New York: Dramatis Play Services, Inc., 2002.

Lord Tennyson, Alfred. "Ulysses." In *The Complete Works of Alfred Tennyson.* New York: R. Worthington, 1879.

Maimonides. *Guide of the Perplexed, Volume 3.* Translated by Shlomo Pines. Chicago: University of Chicago Press, 1963.

Mandela, Nelson. *Long Walk to Freedom.* New York: Little Brown and Company, 1994.

Manent, Pierre. *A World Beyond Politics? A Defense of the Nation State.* Princeton: Princeton University Press, 2006.

Melville, Herman. *Moby-Dick; or, The Whale.* Berkley: University of California Press, 1979.

Mencken, H. L. *Minority Report: H.L. Mencken's Notebooks.* New York: Alfred A. Knopf, 1956.

Merton, Thomas, cited in Matthew Fox. "A Spirituality Called Compassion." *Religious Education* 73, 3, (1978): 284–300.

Mumford, Lewis. *Herman Melville.* New York: Literary Guild of America, 1929.

Nehru, Jawaharlal. *Excerpts from His Writings and Speeches.* Delhi: Ministry of Information and Broadcasting, Government of India, 1964.

Nietzsche, Friedrich. *Basic Writings of Nietzsche.* Translated by Walter Kaufmann. New York: Random House, 2009.

———. *On the Genealogy of Morals.* Edited by Keith Ansell-Pearson. Translated by Carol Diethe. New York: Cambridge University Press, 2007.

———. *On the Genealogy of Morals and Ecce Homo.* Translated by Walter Kaufmann. New York: Vintage, 2010.

Ordoubadian, Reza, trans. *The Poems of Hafez*. Bethesda, Maryland: Ibex Publishers, 2006.

Orwell, George. "Notes on Nationalism." In *England Your England and Other Essays*. London: Secker & Warburg, 1953.

Pearce, Joseph. "An Interview with Alexander Solzhenitsyn." *St. Austin Review* 2 no. 2 (February, 2003): 18–20.

Rawls, John. *A Theory of Justice*. Cambridge, MA: Harvard University Press, 1971.

Ricoeur, Paul. "Forward." In Stephen Strasser, *Phenomenology of Feeling*. Pittsburgh: Duquesne University Press, 1977.

Ricoeur, Paul. *The Symbolism of Evil*. New York: Harper and Row, 1967.

Sampson, Anthony. *Mandela: The Authorized Biography*. New York: Harper Collins, 1999.

Santayana, George. *Reason in Common Sense*. New York: Scribner, 1929.

Sartre, Jean-Paul. "Herman Melville's *Moby Dick*." In *Twentieth-Century Interpretations of Moby Dick*, edited by Michael Gilbert, 94–97. Englewood Cliffs, NJ: Prentice-Hall, 1977.

Scheler, Max. *On Feeling, Knowing, and Valuing: Selected Writings*. Edited by Harold Bershady. Chicago: University of Chicago Press, 1992.

Schopenhauer, Arthur. *On the Basis of Morality*. Translated by E. F. J. Payne. Indianapolis: Bobbs-Merrill, 1965.

——. *The World as Will and Representation*. Translated by E. F. J. Payne. Vol. 1. New York: Dover Publications, Inc., 1969.

Shakespeare, William. *The Norton Shakespeare, Second Edition*. Edited by Stephen Greenblatt. New York: W.W. Norton & Company, 2008.

Shaw, George Bernard. *Androcles and the Lion*. London: Penguin Books, 1957.

Slights, William W. E. "The Sacrificial Crisis in *Titus Andronicus*." *University of Toronto Quarterly* 49, no. 1 (1979): 18–32.

Solzhenitsyn, Alexander. *One Word of Truth*. London: Bodley Head, 1972.

Sophocles. *The Three Theban Plays: Antigone, Opedipus the King, Oedipus at Colonus.* Translated by Robert Fagles. London: Penguin Classics, 1984.

Stevenson, Angus, ed. *The Oxford Dictionary of English.* Oxford: Oxford University Press, 2010.

Stirner, Max. *The Ego and Its Own.* New York: Boni and Liveright, Inc., 1918.

Szasz, Thomas. *The Second Sin.* New York: Doubleday, 1973.

The Holy Bible: New King James Version. New York: Harper Collins, 1982.

Thoreau, Henry David. "Civil Disobedience." In *Walden, Civil Disobedience, and Other Writings.* Edited by Owen Thomas. New York: W.W. Norton, 2008.

———. *A Year in Thoreau's Journal: 1851.* New York: Penguin Books, 1993.

Todorov, Tzvetan. *Facing the Extreme: Moral Life in the Concentration Camps.* Translated by Arthur Denner and Abigail Pollak. New York: Metropolitan Books, 1996.

Trend, John Brande. *Lorca and the Spanish Poetic Tradition.* Oxford: Russell & Russell, 1956.

Tutu, Desmond. *No Future without Forgiveness.* New York, Doubleday, 1999.

Udoff, Alan, ed. *Vladimir Jankélévitch and the Question of Forgiveness.* Lanham: Lexington Books, 2013.

Williams, Robert R. *Hegel's Ethics of Recognition.* Berkeley: University of California Press, 1997.

"Words of the Week." *Jet* 34, no. 11 (20 June 1968): 30.

Yeats, William Butler. *Responsibilities, and other poems.* New York: MacMillan, 1916.

Zorba the Greek. Directed by Michael Cacoyannis. 1964. Burbank, CA: 20th Century Fox, 2004.

ABOUT THE AUTHOR

THE WINNER OF THE PEACE PRIZE FROM the United Nations in Spain and an advisory board member of PEN Canada, Ramin Jahanbegloo is an internationally celebrated philosopher and author whose books are published around the world. He is currently York-Noor Visiting Chair in Islamic Studies at York University in Toronto.

THE REGINA COLLECTION

Named as a tribute to Saskatchewan's capital city with its rich history of boundary-defying innovation, The Regina Collection builds upon University of Regina Press's motto of "a voice for many peoples." Intimate in size and beautifully packaged, these books aim to tell the stories of those who have been caught up in social and political circumstances beyond their control.

A NOTE ON THE TYPE

THIS BOOK IS SET IN ADOBE CASLON PRO, A variant of the work of William Caslon, and designed by Carol Twombly in 1990 for Adobe Systems. Caslon, who released his first typefaces in 1722, based his work on seventeenth-century Dutch old style designs, which were then used extensively in England. Because of their remarkable practicality, Caslon's designs met with instant success and became popular throughout Europe and the American colonies. For her Caslon revival, Twombly studied specimen pages printed by William Caslon between 1734 and 1770.

Text and cover design by Duncan Campbell, University of Regina Press.